Some Lessons in Metaphysics

JOSÉ ORTEGA Y GASSET

BORN IN MADRID IN 1883, José Ortega y Gasset was one of the intellectual leaders of the Spanish Republican government. After the establishment of the Republic, Ortega became a member of Parliament. He also held for many years the chair of metaphysics at the University of Madrid and was editor of the influential journal of opinion, *Revista de Occidente*. After the Spanish Civil War, Ortega became an exile from Spain, living for a time in Buenos Aires, later settling in Lisbon. In recent years he visited Spain to lecture in Madrid. *Man and Crisis* was originally published in Spanish under the title of *En Torno A Galileo*. Other books by Ortega include his most widely read work *The Revolt of the Masses, Man and People, Meditations on Quixote, History as a System, What Is Philosophy?, Mission of the University,* and *The Origin of Philosophy.* Señor Ortega died in 1955.

"Ortega y Gasset, after Nietzsche, is perhaps
the greatest 'European' writer."
                                        —ALBERT CAMUS

by JOSÉ ORTEGA Y GASSET

JOSÉ ORTEGA Y GASSET

SOME
LESSONS IN
METAPHYSICS

TRANSLATED BY MILDRED ADAMS

W · W · NORTON & COMPANY · INC · New York

864
Or 8
KAd19s

SBN 393 08591 0

FIRST EDITION

1 2 3 4 5 6 7 8 9 0

Note by the Spanish Publishers

THE TEXT which is here transcribed comes from one of Ortega's manuscripts and presents the course which he gave when he occupied the Chair of Metaphysics at the University of Madrid in 1932–33. Ortega's explanations in class led him at times, and for reasons of circumstance, to complementary developments of his subject, but the text printed here contains only the manuscript as he prepared it for the lessons, as it was found among his papers.

For recent generations who were never able to attend his classes, these pages present an opportunity to watch the creation and formulations of an original trend of thought which for twenty-five years raised the teaching of philosophy in the Spanish university to its greatest heights.

Translator's Preface

José Ortega y Gasset, who was Spain's most famous modern philosopher, died more than a dozen years ago, but his words and the thoughts within them go marching on. In a country that, until very recently, lived as much to itself as though it were on the African side of the Straits of Gibraltar, he was one of very few writers who made any real impression outside the Spanish borders. His fame in the United States came with the publishing of that far-sighted volume of social analysis and prophecy, *The Revolt of the Masses;* this he followed with a dozen other volumes illuminating the major problems that obsess us all. Some of these have yet to appear in the dress of English prose.

Ortega was a writer and a thinker in the finest sense— his philosophy occupies philosophers and his Spanish style is an artistic creation that defies any adequate equivalent in English. He was also an extraordinary educator who attracted crowded classes of eager students and filled lecture halls with enthusiasts of all ages. His inexhaustible subject was some phase of man and his problems. Academic posts of great distinction which he occupied did not give sufficient outlet for his intense desire to make basic subjects clear and interesting to the average man. This passion infused his activities as a journalist. His father had been a newspaper publisher, and Ortega's entry into the writing world came by way of newspaper pages where he wrote essays that are still read by oncoming generations seeking meaningful revelations and interpretations of the world they are just beginning to discover. He wrote on love and bullfighting, on hunting

9

and education, as well as on Don Quixote; his incessant search for knowledge led him into political theory and practice, as well as into metaphysics.

This present book represents Ortega's incursions into a field of thought that most Americans consider a closed region for the average man. Yet anyone curious enough to travel along with this clear light of the Ortega mind will find himself led into a succession of ideas that extend his vision and his understanding of himself. From the days of the Greeks, generations of men have puzzled over man's role in the universe and have tried to put it into words. Ortega accomplishes this in one pregnant phrase which is found in this book, "I am myself and my circumstances" (the things around me); and it is so simple and appealingly true that it may come as a great surprise to find it hailed as an important philosophic contribution. In this day of alienation, when the young have difficulty finding out who or what they are, Ortega's venture into metaphysics is a lit lamp in a continuing darkness. His discussion, in the first lesson, of the student's role as it really is will shed a long light on the reasons for present student disorders.

M.A.

Some Lessons in Metaphysics

Lesson I

The false elements in studying. Metaphysics and the need for it. Antagonism between the student and the creator of science. Curiosity and preoccupation. The tragedy of pedagogy. Culture without roots; a return to barbarity. Question and answer. "Doing" and the justification of metaphysics.

I HOPE THAT during this course you will come to a complete understanding of the first phrase which, after these introductory words, I am about to pronounce [1].

The phrase is this: we are going to study metaphysics, and in what we are going to do there is, for the moment, an element of falseness. At first sight, this idea is stupefying; but the stupor produced by the phrase does not take from it the dose of truth that is in it. In that phrase —note it well—we do not say that metaphysics may be false; this characteristic is attributed not to metaphysics, but to the fact that we are setting out to study it. We are not discussing a false element in any of our thoughts, but a false quality in one of the things that we are doing—the studying of a discipline. Because what I am saying, eminently valid for metaphysics, is valid for more than that; according to this, studying, in general, would be a deception.

1. The first pages of this lesson were published under the title 'On Studying and the Student' in *Obras Completas* [Ortega's complete works], vol. IV. The epigraphs heading the lessons were edited by the compilers [*Compilers' note*]. Ortega left a vast mass of papers, some ready for publishing and others not. His family entrusted the task of sorting, etc. to a group of close co-workers and followers who, in preparing works for publication, called themselves the 'compilers' and occasionally wrote explanatory notes in that name [*Translator's note*].

Such a phrase and a thesis would hardly seem the most opportune for a professor to offer his students, especially at the beginning of a course. These may sound like phrases advocating flight, absence, like recommendations that you go away and not come back. We will see about that: see whether you do go away, whether you fail to come back for the reason that I have begun by stating a sizeable pedagogical enormity.

It may be that the very opposite will happen; you may find yourselves interested by this unheard-of assertion. While one thing or another is happening, while you are making up your minds to go or to stay, I am going to clarify the meaning of the phrase.

I did not say that studying would be only a deception and nothing else; it may have facets, sides, ingredients that may not be false. But for me, the fact that some of the facets, sides, or essential ingredients of studying are false is enough to give my statement its own truth.

This last seems to me beyond dispute. For one simple reason. The disciplines—whether they be metaphysics or geometry—exist. They are here because men created them by brute force, and if they used that force, it was because they needed those disciplines so badly that they had to have them.

The truths that these disciplines might contain were found in the first place by one man, and were then re-thought or rediscovered by others who added their own efforts to that of the first man. But if they found these truths, it is because they sought them, and if they sought them, it is because men had need of them, because for one reason or another they could not do without them.

And if they had not found them, those men would have considered their lives to be ruined. If, on the other hand, they found what they sought, it is evident that what they found was adequate to the need they felt. This, which is a commonplace, is nevertheless very important. We say that we have discovered a truth when we have found a certain thought that satisfies an intellectual need which we have previously felt. If we do not feel in need of that thought, it will not be a truth for us. Truth, for the moment, is what quiets an anxiety in our intelligence. Without this anxiety there is no place for this quieting. Similarly, we say that we have found the key when we have found a precise object which makes it possible for us to open a closet that we need to open. The exact search is soothed by the precise finding; the latter is the function of the former.

If we make the expression general, we will find that a truth does not properly exist except for the one who has need of it, that a science is not such except for one who seeks it eagerly, in short, that metaphysics is not metaphysics except for those who need it.

For one who does not need it, who does not seek it, metaphysics is a series of words or, if you like, a series of ideas which, although they are each thought to have been understood, definitely lack meaning; in order truly to understand something, and most of all metaphysics, it is not necessary to have what is called talent or to possess great prior wisdom. On the other hand, what is essential is a condition that is elementary but fundamental; what is necessary is to have need of metaphysics.

But there are various forms of wanting, of need to the point of beggary. If someone forces me inexorably to do something, I will necessarily do it. Yet this need to do is not mine; it did not surge up in me, but was imposed on me from the outside. For example, I feel the need of walking and this need arises within me—which is not to say that it is a whim, or a matter of taste. No. Besides being a need, it has about it something of an imposition in that it does not originate in my free will but is imposed on me from within my being; I feel it, in effect, as a necessity of *my own*. But when, on my going out to walk, the traffic officer makes me follow a certain route, I find myself with another need, one which is not mine, but comes to me imposed from the outside, and the only thing that I can do about it is to convince myself of its advantages by reflecting on them and, in view of them, to accept them. But to accept a necessity, to recognize it, is not to feel it, not to feel it immediately as a need of my own; rather, it is a necessity of things which comes to me from them, an alien need and strange to me. We will call this the mediate necessity, as contrasted with the immediate, which I feel as a necessity born within me, having its roots in me, indigenous, autochthonous, authentic.

There is an expression of St. Francis of Assisi wherein both forms of need appear subtly counterposed. St. Francis was accustomed to say, 'I need little, and that little I need very little'. In the first part of the phrase, St. Francis alludes to the external or mediate needs; in the second, to the intimate, authentic, and immediate needs. Like all living men, St. Francis needed to eat in order to live, but in him, this external need was very slender; that is to say, he needed materially to eat little in order to live. But, in addition, his intimate attitude was that he felt no great need to live; that is, he felt very little attachment to life and, consequently, very little intimate necessity for the external need of eating.

Well now, when man sees himself obliged to accept an external and mediate need, he finds himself in an equivocal, ambivalent situation, because this is the same as being invited to make his own (which means to accept) a necessity which is not his. Whether he likes it or not, he must behave *as though* it were his; he is thus invited to share in a fiction, a falsehood, a deception. And although this man may put forth all his good will in order to feel *as if* it were his, this does not mean that he achieves this, nor is it even probable that he can.

Having made this clear, let us turn our attention to the normal situation of the man who is called on to study, if we use this word as meaning the studying that a student does; or, what is the same thing, let us ask ourselves what

a student is. And the fact is that we then find ourselves
with something as startling as was the scandalous phrase
with which I began this course. We find ourselves faced
with the fact that the student is a human being, male or
female, on whom life imposes the need to study sciences
for which he has felt no immediate, genuine need. Leaving aside the cases that are exceptional, we recognize that
in the best of cases the student feels a sincere, if somewhat vague, need to study 'something', thus, *in genere* 'to
know', to be instructed. But the vagueness of this wish
testifies to its slender stock of authenticity. It is evident
that such a state of mind has never led to the creation of
any real knowledge, because such knowledge is always
concrete, a matter of the precise knowing of this or that;
and, according to the law (at which I have barely hinted)
of the functional relationship between seeking and finding, need and satisfaction, those who created knowledge
felt no vague desire for knowing, but a most concrete
and specific desire to find out this or that specific thing.

This shows that even in the best of cases—and again, I
repeat, saving exceptions—the desire to know, which the
good student may feel, is completely heterogeneous and
perhaps even antagonistic to the state of mind which led
to the creation of a particular order of knowledge. Thus,
the attitude of the student toward science is the opposite
of that which stirred its creator. As a matter of fact,
science does not exist in advance of its creator. He did
not first find it and then feel the need to possess it; he
first felt a need that was vital rather than scientific, and
this led him to seek the satisfaction of that need. In finding this in certain ideas, the result was that these were the
science.

The student, on the other hand, finds himself with the
science already made, as with a mountain range that rises
in front of him and cuts off his vital road. In the best of
cases, I repeat, the mountain range of science pleases him,
attracts him, seems good to him, promises him victories

in life. But none of this has anything to do with the genuine need which led originally to the creation of this science. The proof of this lies in the fact that the general desire to know is incapable of becoming concrete in the sense of a strict desire for knowledge in a specific field. Apart, I repeat, from the fact that it is not desire which leads to knowledge, but necessity. The desire does not exist unless the thing desired existed earlier, in reality or at least in imagination. That which does not even exist at all cannot provoke desire. Our desires are fired by contact with what is already here. On the other hand, a genuine need can exist without there having to pre-exist—even in imagaination—the thing which might satisfy it. One needs precisely what one does not have, what is lacking, what is not existent, and the need, the demand, is that much stronger the less one has, the less there is of what is required.

In order to see this clearly, we need not depart from our theme. It is enough to compare the approach of a man who is going to study an already-existing science with the approach of a man who feels a real, sincere, and genuine need for it. The former will tend not to question the content of the science not to criticize it; on the contrary, he will tend to comfort himself by thinking that the content of the science which already exists has a defined value, is pure truth. What he seeks is simply to assimilate it as it already is. On the other hand, the man who is needful of a science, he who feels the profound necessity of truth, will approach this bit of ready-made knowledge with caution, full of suspicion and prejudice, submitting it to criticism, even assuming in advance that what the book says is not true. In short, for the very reason that he needs, with such deep anguish, to know, he will think that this knowledge does not exist, and he will manage to unmake what is presented as already made. It is men like this who are constantly correcting, renewing, recreating science.

But that is not, in the normal sense of the term, what the student's studying means. If the science were not already there, the good student would not feel the need of it, which means that he would not be a student. Therefore, the matter is an external need which is imposed upon him. To put a man in the position of a student is to oblige him to undertake something false, to pretend that he feels a need which he does not feel.

But there are objections that will be made to this. It will, for example, be said that there are students who deeply feel the need to solve certain problems that are involved in this science or that. Certainly there are people like that, but it is hardly sound to call them students. It is not only unsound, it is unjust. Because these are the exceptional cases of creatures who, even if there were neither studies nor science, would, by themselves, invent them for better or for worse, and would by the force of an inexorable vocation, dedicate their strength to investigating them. But . . . the others? The immense and normal majority? It is they, and not those other more venturesome ones, who bring into being the true meaning— not the utopian meaning—of the words 'student' and 'to study'. It is unjust not to recognize them as the real students, and unjust not to question with respect to them the problem of what studying as a form and type of human occupation, is.

It is an imperative of our time—I will later explain the serious reasons for this—that we think things through to their naked, factual, and dramatic selves. This is the only way of coming face to face with them. It would be delightful if being a student were to mean feeling a most lively desire for this, that, or the other kind of knowledge. But the truth is exactly the opposite; to be a student is to see oneself as the person obliged to interest himself in the very thing that does not interest him or, at best, interests him only vaguely, indirectly, or in general terms.

The other objection one would have to make comes from remembering that boys and girls do feel a sincere curiosity and have their own enthusiastic preferences. The student is not a student in general, but one who studies science or letters; and this assumes a predisposition of mind, a hunger which is less vague and not imposed from the outside.

In the nineteenth century, too much importance was given to curiosity and enthusiastic preferences; there was a desire to base on these emotions things that were too serious, too weighty to be supported by entities as unserious as those were.

This word 'curiosity', like so many other words, has a double meaning, one primary and of substance, the other pejorative and abusive, like the word "aficionado" which means both one who truly loves something, and also one who is merely an *amateur*. The true meaning of the word 'curiosity' stems from a Latin root (Heidegger recently called our attention to this), the word *cura*, meaning the cared for, the *cares*, what I call preoccupation. From *cura* comes *curiosity*. Hence, in daily speech, a curious man is a careful man, a man who does what he has to do with attention, extreme care, and precision, a man who neither slights nor neglects whatever occupies him, but, on the contrary, is preoccupied with his occupations. Even in ancient Spanish, *cuidar* meant to be occupied, to *care*. This original meaning of *cura* (care) or *cuidados* (cares) survives in our present terms *curador* (overseer), *procurator* (procuror), *procurar* (to procure), *curar* (to cure), and in the very word *cura* (curate) which is given to the priest because he has the care of souls. Curiosity, then, is carefulness, preoccupation. And, vice versa, *incuria* is carelessness, lack of interest, and *seguridad* (security), *securitas*, is the absence of cares or of preoccupations.

If, for example, I search for the keys, it is because I am preoccupied with them, and if I am preoccupied with them, it is because I need them in order to do something, to occupy myself.

When this preoccupation is exercised mechanically, without sincerity or a sufficent motive, and it degenerates into a mere appetite, we have a human vice that consists in pretending care for what, in fact, we do not care about, in a false concern with things that are not truly going to occupy us, and, therefore, in becoming incapable of genuine preoccupation. And that is what the expressions 'curiosity', 'being curious', and 'being a curious one' mean when used in their pejorative sense.

So when it is said that curiosity leads us to this science or that, we may either be talking about that sincere preoccupation with science which I earlier called 'immediate and inborn need' (this, we recognize, is not usually felt by the student) or we refer to the frivolously curious, to the appetite for putting one's nose into everything; this, I think, could hardly serve to make a man a scientist.

These objections are, for the moment, inane. Let us not go further with idealizations of the harsh reality, with cherished ideas that induce us to weaken, to soften, to blur the edges of the problems; let us not put balls on the bull's horns. The fact is that the typical student is one who does not feel the direct need of a science, nor any real concern with it, and who yet sees himself forced to busy himself with it. This indicates the general deception which surrounds studying. But then comes the stiffening of that deception, almost perverse in its effect, for it does not lead the student to study in general, but to study broken into sectors leading to careers, with each career made up of individual disciplines, of this science or that. And who is going to pretend that a lad, at a certain year of his life, is going to feel the effective need of a science which his predecessors were moved to invent out of their own necessities?

Thus, out of so genuine and lively a need that men—the creators of science—dedicated their entire lives to it, is made a dead need and a false activity. Let us not spin illusions; in that state of mind, human attempts at learning cannot reach the stage of human knowing. To study, then, is something fundamentally false and contradictory. The student is a falsification of the man. Because man *is* properly no more than he genuinely is, out of his own intimate and inexorable necessity. To be a man is to be, to do only what he irremediably is. And there are an infinite number of ways of being a man, and all of them are equally genuine. One can be a man of science, or a business man, or a political man, or a religious man, because all these, as we will see, are constitutional and immediate needs of the human condition. But man by himself would never be a student, just as man by himself would never be a tax-payer. He *must* pay taxes, he *has* to study, but he *is* by nature neither a taxpayer nor a student. To be a student or to be a taxpayer is an artificial state in which man finds himself by obligation.

This, which may have sounded so stupefying when we first pronounced it, becomes the essential tragedy of the teaching profession, and in my judgment, the reform of education ought to begin with that brutal paradox.

Because the activity itself—the activity which pedagogy regulates and which we call studying—is humanly false, something happens that is not as much emphasized as it should be; namely, that in no order of life is the element of falsity so constant, so habitual, and so tolerated as it is in teaching. I know full well that justice also may be false, and that abuses are committed in the courts. But weigh the comparison for yourselves, out of your own experience, and tell me if we would not be quite content if there did not exist within the teaching activity any greater inadequacy and abuse than are suffered in the juridical order? What is considered in the courts as intolerable abuse—that justice not be done—is in teaching almost the norm: the student does not study, and if he does, putting his best will into it, he does not learn; and it is clear that if the student, for whatever reason, does not learn, the professor cannot say that he is teaching; at the very best, he is trying to teach but is not succeeding.

Meanwhile, generation after generation, the frightening mass of human knowledge which the student must assimilate piles up. And in proportion, as knowledge grows, is enriched, and becomes specialized, the student will move farther and farther away from feeling any immediate and genuine need for it. Each time, there will be less congruence between the sad human activity which is studying, and the admirable human occupation which is true knowing. And so the terrible gap which began at least a century ago continues to grow, the gap between living culture, genuine knowledge, and the ordinary man. Since culture or knowledge has no other reality than to respond to needs that are truly felt and to satisfy them in one way or another, while the way of transmitting knowledge is to study, which is not to feel those needs, what we have is that culture or knowledge hangs in mid-air and has no roots of sincerity in the average man who finds himself forced to swallow it whole. That is to say, there is introduced into the human mind a foreign body, a set of dead ideas that could not be assimilated.

This culture, which does not have any root structure in man, a culture which does not spring from him spontaneously, lacks any native and indigenous values; this is something imposed, extrinsic, strange, foreign, and unintelligible; in short, it is unreal. Underneath this culture—received but not truly assimilated—man will remain intact as he was; that is to say, he will remain uncultured, a barbarian. When the process of knowing was shorter, more elemental, and more organic, it came closer to being felt by the common man who then assimilated it, recreated it, and revitalized it within himself. This explains the colossal paradox of these decades—that an enormous progress in terms of culture should have pro-

duced a man of the type we now have, a man indis-
putably more barbarous than was the man of a hundred
years ago; and that this acculturation, this accumulation
of culture, should produce—paradoxically but automatically—humanity's return to barbarism.

You will understand that the problem is not solved by
saying, 'All right, but if studying is a falsifying of man,
and if, in addition, it leads, or can lead, to such consequences, let us not study'. To say this would not be to
solve the problem, but simply to ignore it. To study and
to be a student was always, and is now above all, one of
man's inexorable needs. Whether he wants to or not, he
has to assimilate the accumulation of knowledge under
pain of succumbing, either as an individual or as a group.
If a whole generation should cease to study, nine-tenths
of the human race then alive would die a violent death.
The number of men now living can continue to subsist
only by virtue of the superior techniques of making
good use of the planet that the sciences make possible.
Techniques can be taught, mechanically. But techniques
live on knowing, and if this cannot be taught, an hour
will come in which the techniques too will succumb.

So one must study. This, I repeat, is one of man's
needs, but it is an external, mediate necessity like moving
to the right as the traffic officer directs when I need to go
walking. But between the two external necessities—
studying and moving to the right—there is an essential
difference which is the thing that converts study into a
substantive problem. In order for traffic to function perfectly, it is not necessary that I feel an intimate need to
go to the right; it is enough that I do, in fact, move in
that direction, that I accept the need for this, that I pretend to feel it. But it is not the same with study; in order
for me truly to understand a science, it is not enough for
me to pretend the need for it within myself; or, what is
the same thing, it is not enough that I have the will to
accept it; in short, it is not enough that I study. It is also

necessary that I should genuinely feel the need of this, that I be spontaneously and truly preoccupied with its questions; only then will I understand the answers it gives or tries to give. No one can thoroughly understand an answer unless he has understood the question to which it replies.

In this way, the case of studying is different from that of walking to the right. In the latter, to achieve the anticipated effect, it is sufficient that I do it well. In the former, this is not so; to succeed in assimilating a science, it is not enough for me to be a good student. Therefore, we have in this something man does which contradicts itself; it is at once both necessary and useless. Man must do it in order to achieve a certain end, but the result is that he fails to succeed. Because both things—its necessity and its lack of utility—are equally true, studying is a problem. A problem is always a contradiction which intelligence finds facing it, a contradiction which pulls it in two opposite directions and threatens to tear it apart.

The solution to so crude a two-horned problem may be inferred from what I have said; it does not consist of decreeing that one not study, but of a deep reform of that human activity called studying and, hence, of the student's being. In order to achieve this, one must turn teaching completely around and say that primarily and fundamentally teaching is only the teaching of a need for the science and *not* the teaching of the science itself whose need the student does not feel.

PERHAPS some of you have been asking yourselves, 'What has all this to do with a course in metaphysics?'. I hope— and I began with this—that during this course you will understand not only what the previously-mentioned matters have to do with metaphysics, but also that we are already in the midst of it. But for the moment, let us give a clearer justification of having begun this way, antici-

pating a first definition of metaphysics, the one that looks
to be most modest, the one that no one will dare invali-
date. Let us say that metaphysics is something that man
does, something man makes—at least some men; later, we
will see whether or not all men do it, even though they
might not be aware of it. But this definition is not sufficient, for man does many things, and not merely metaphysics; indeed, man is an incessant, inescapable, pure
doer. He makes his house, he makes politics, he makes in-
dustry, he makes verses, he makes science, he creates pa-
tience, and at the very moment that he seems to be doing
nothing, he is in fact waiting, hoping, and your experience will confirm the fact that waiting and hoping is a
terrible and most anguished process; it is making time [2].
And he who neither waits nor hopes, the *faitnéant*, he
who truly does nothing, makes that nothing; that is to
say, he sustains and supports the nothing which lies
within himself, that terrible, vital emptiness which we
call boredom, *spleen*, desperation. He who does not hope
despairs—a form of activity that is so horrible, requiring
so wild a force, that it is one of those which man can
least exhaust; he usually carries it to the extreme of making an actual and absolute nothing, of destroying himself,
of committing suicide.

Among such varied and omnigenous activities, how
can we recognize the one that is certainly metaphysical?
For this, we will have to put forth a second and more
precise definition: man engages in metaphysics when he
seeks a basic orientation in his situation.

But what is man's situation? He finds himself not in
one, but in many different situations; for example, you
find yourselves in one now. You happen to be in the situation of setting out to study metaphysics; two hours ago,

2. The Spanish phrase *hacer tiempo*, to make time, is the Spanish
equivalent of the English phrase 'to kill time'. The difference
between these two verbal descriptions of the same act is worth
noting for anyone trying to understand the two peoples [*Translator's note*].

you found yourselves in another situation, and tomorrow you will be in still another. Now, all these situations, however different they may be, coincide in being parts of your lives. Man's life seems to be made up of situations, just as matter is composed of atoms. As long as one lives, one is living in a specific situation. But it is evident that just as all these situations, however different they may be, are vital, so there will be in them an elemental, basic structure which makes all of them situations within the realm of man. That generic structure will be made up of what they have in essence of human life. Or to put it another way, whatever may be the varied and variable ingredients which form the situation in which I find myself, it is evident that that situation will be me living. Therefore, man's primary situation is life, is living.

And we say that metaphysics consists of the fact that man seeks a basic orientation in his situation. But this assumes that man's situation—that is, his life—consists of a basic disorientation. This is not a matter of man's finding himself, in his own life, partly disoriented in this or that respect—in his business, or in his strolling through the countryside, or in politics. He who is disoriented in the country looks at a map or a compass, or questions a passerby, and this is enough to put him right. But our definition presupposes a total and fundamental dislocation; that is to say, it is not that man happens to be disoriented, to be losing himself in life, but that, insofar as one can see, man's situation, his life, in itself *is* disorientation, is being lost, and, therefore, metaphysics exists.

Lesson II

Metaphysics and basic orientation. Genuine orientation and fictitious orientation. The person himself and the conventional personality. Life is what we do and what happens to us. The attributes of life. Life is evidential. The world is what affects us. Life is always unforeseen. To live is to feel ourselves forced to decide what we are going to be. To live is, above all, to collide with the future.

METAPHYSICS is something that man does, and that doing consists of his seeking a basic orientation in his situation. This seems to imply that man's situation is a fundamental disorientation or, what is the same thing, that being oriented is not one of the constituent attributes belonging to the essence of man, to his true being; on the contrary, the human essence is man's basic lack of orientation in life.

Perhaps—note that I say no more than 'perhaps'—what I call the oriented man is what is traditionally called 'knowing what things are', 'knowing the score'. Why not use this customary phrase? As a matter of fact, he who knows what things are, who 'knows the score'—taking the term 'things' in its broadest and vaguest sense—is oriented. In this sense, orientation would be no more than knowing, or being acquainted with. But apart from the fact that this is not certain (as we will see in a moment), note the change which it would produce in our definition. If we substitute 'knowing' for 'orientation', we would have metaphysics as the basic knowing.

Now, this definition assumes that we all know what knowing is—both knowing and knowing about [1]—other-

1. Spanish has two words for the English 'to know'—*saber* which implies knowledge, wisdom, and *conocer* which means to be ac-

wise we would not use the term. As a matter of fact, it has been philosophy's continual habit to assume that everyone knows what knowing is, what the being of things is, and that knowledge consists in taking possession of these. But it is my precise intent to discuss philosophic problems on a deeper level than the one on which they have customarily been attacked. I do not take it for granted that knowing and being are as they are generally assumed and understood to be, and I do not make metaphysics consist merely of setting forth to find out what things are, believing that if I find this out I then *know;* given that the traditional idea of knowing, or knowledge, consists of a person's intellectual possession of the being of things. The truth is that I can only find out lamely what things are if I do not previously know what being is. If I do not know what being is, how will I know what the being of things is?

We have, then, the fact that these two reciprocal ideas —being and knowing, or knowing about—always loom in the background behind metaphysics or philosophy. Yet for a century and a half, the theory of knowledge was considered as an initial and fundamental part of philosophy, just as for a thousand years, the initial or fundamental part of philosophy was considered to be ontology, or the theory of being. How, then, can I assert that to pose as problems 'what is knowing' and 'what is being' constitutes an innovation if these are the two classic and canonical questions of all philosophy? But this is the wonderful thing about the matter; up to now, when philosophy studied being, what it was studying was the being of things; it asked, 'What are things?', but it did not ask, 'What is being?'. This it took for granted; it did not make a question out of it, but left it behind. And similarly, when the theory of knowledge asked itself, 'What

quainted with. Ortega uses both with a discrimination hard to approximate with the single English 'to know' [*Translator's note*].

is knowing or knowing about?', what it sought to find
out was 'if it was possible, *how* it was possible, *what* its
limits and norms were'. But it never occurred to philosophers or to theorists to view the question in its most
obvious, basic, and primary sense, namely, 'What is this
whose possibility, functioning, limits, and norms we are
investigating?'. Or to put it another way, they did not
ask, 'How is it that there exists in the universe this something that we call knowing? What is its primary meaning? Of what does it consist?'—and do this before they
asked about its possibility, its functioning, and so on.

If 'knowing' and 'being' are the two basic problems, to
define metaphysics as basic knowing is to take this as already presupposed; even worse, it is to leave the most
important part of it at the door, and to begin when
everything is already accepted as solved. As for me, I
aspire to take philosophy on a level which is earlier and
deeper than the one which was cultivated by the past.
Unlike the sciences, philosophy does not progress in a
horizontal dimension by means of successive broaden-
ings. It progresses downward toward the depths, and its
advance consists in questioning that which previously
had not been questionable.

As we will see, the idea of orientation is more basic,
deeper, and earlier than the idea of knowing, and not the
opposite. Being oriented is not made truly clear by the
concept of knowing; orientation is not a form of knowing, but, on the contrary, knowing is a form of orientation.

Having said this, let us turn to the definition of metaphysics as what man does when he seeks a fundamental
orientation in his situation. This assumes, we were saying,
that man's situation is disorientation. Well now, it is almost certain that all of you have felt yourselves to be
more or less oriented. Consequently, you do not need to
engage in metaphysics, nor can you. But the definition
implies something more serious. It does not say that man

creates metaphysics when his situation is one of disorientation, and only then—admitting, therefore, that he can find himself in other situations where he is oriented—but it affirms, in a limited way, the view that man's situation is always one of disorientation. One can say 'disorientation', or 'feeling lost'—it is the same. The definition assumes, then, that man feels himself lost not merely from time to time but all the time, or, what is the same thing, that man consists in substance of feeling himself lost.

Now, I suspect that not one of you feels lost. Therefore, my definition in this area, which is the decisive one, expresses a crass error. Do not, however, jump to the conclusion that this means that of all those who are here, I am the only one who feels lost, with the result that the only lost one is the metaphysician and that, therefore, it is he who needs metaphysics.

To feel oneself lost! Did you ever consider what those words mean in themselves? Without going beyond them, to feel oneself lost implies first the sensation of feeling oneself—that is, meeting oneself, finding oneself; but, by the same token, that self which man encounters on feeling himself consists precisely in a pure state of being lost.

Well then, if you each turn your attention inward toward yourself, you will not find yourself in a situation of loss and disorientation, but just the opposite. You each find yourself installed in a lecture hall in the Central University, an edifice and an institution which belong to the Spanish land and nation; this land and nation form part of a planet whose dimensions and location in the astronomic cosmos are well known to you; or, if not, you are sure that whenever you might need to know this, you could quickly find it out. All that and much more—for example, the constituent materials of which that astronomic cosmos is made, the laws of its behavior, and so on—is familiar to you in general or in some detail. In another sphere, it is well known to each of you that your own person is made up of a thing called 'soul' and another thing called 'body', whose condition—at least in their principal attributes—form part of your intellectual possessions; in short, you know them. We could go on indefinitely making an inventory of all the components of your situation which are familiar to you.

It is possible that something even more decisive for the effects of your orientation is completely familiar to some of you; namely, that in addition to your body and your soul and the physical cosmos, there exists a personal *Ente*, a Being, the creator of all this, omnipotent, infinitely wise and good, who communicates with man and directs him by means of revelation, thus making possible an absolute orientation. Can one ask for more?

And it is a fact that day after day you lead your own existence, setting it in motion amid the things that are familiar to it, behaving in each of your actions in accordance with the orientation which all these constants prescribe. Not one of you will try to leave this hall through the wall, because it is clear to you that the wall is very hard and to be perforated only with difficulty. In view of this, you will manage to find the door, because it is clear to you that the door is an object through which you can go. This is so humble, so elemental, a constant that it becomes ridiculous to point it out; but, by the same token, it shows somewhat crudely up to what point the need for orientation is basic, in that our most humble and elemental acts presuppose it.

To say that something 'is clear to us' and to say that 'we have a conviction' about something are to say the same thing. I have just alluded briefly to the repertory of convictions you possess which make you feel oriented rather than lost. Among these convictions, let us take one that seems very solid—namely, that 2 and 2 make 4. This is clear and familiar to you. But if we analyze it, we find ourselves facing a surprise. It is probable that not one of you has had any question as to whether 2 and 2 actually make 4 or not. What, then, does it mean when I say that this is clear to you, that you have this conviction? It means that you have received it from your social surroundings, that you have heard it said; it is clear to you only because it is clear to others—for instance, to the mathematicians. Or to put it another way, you have the conviction that others have this conviction; but this means that you yourself are not personally convinced. You make use of that conviction, but it is not yours—you act *as if* it were clear to you. It is a constant that is devoid of effectiveness, a constant that is fictitious; it is in you because it is in others, because it is in the social atmosphere. Vice versa, if some day you ask yourselves whether in fact 2 and 2 really *do* make 4, and after making a question out of it you are, for obvious reasons, effectively convinced that this is so, then it will happen that each one of you will have this conviction, the conviction will be your own and no one else's, in short, that it will be truly clear to every one of you. But note that this effective certainty has come to you because, and only because, you made a question of the matter, and that while the question was being made, the matter, for you, was questionable; or, what is the same thing, you felt yourselves perplexed as to whether 2 and 2 actually did make 4, and in this you were disoriented, lost.

And as the same thing happens with all the other constants and convictions that make up our orientation, whether real or presumed, we come to the conclusion that there are apparently two ways of being oriented or of having things made clear to us; one in which orientation is effective, in which something is made effectively clear to each one of us, to our own selves—but this way always assumes a previous disorientation, a previous lack of clarity. There is also another way, in which orientation is fictitious, in which it is not our own self that is convinced, but a pseudo self which comes to us out of the social fabric; this has dislodged and supplanted our real personality and now acts within us. This fictitious orientation is the one that presupposes no previous disorientation.

What has been said is enough to indicate that man may find himself in one of two situations—an authentic one which implies disorientation and thereby forces us to try to orient ourselves, and another, fictitious and false, in which we think of ourselves as oriented. How is this last one possible? Look at the tremendous thing it signifies. As man conducts his affairs, as he goes on living in view of his orientation, of the repertory of his convictions, all his acts—and, therefore, his whole life—will, in the case of fictitious orientation, be themselves fictitious. And, in fact, if you analyze your own situation, you will note that the type of orientation in which you find yourselves has, in the ultimate depths of your conscience, a character that is provisional. You will also recognize that you have adopted this for the very purpose of avoiding the need to question things; perhaps for the very reason that underneath this mask you have a presentiment of being basically disoriented, lost. This presentiment, this possibility, produces horror in your heart, and you manage to protect yourselves by shifting attention from it and embarking blindly on the vagrant convictions of others, installing yourselves in the commonplace, in what you hear said.

If this analysis which I suggest were certain, it would be equivalent to saying that you are fleeing from your own authentic selves and substituting for them a conventional personality.

But the fact is that I must take you as you are, and you are here where, for the moment, orientation is assumed. That orientation is what makes each of you now feel yourself completely 'found', not 'lost'. In fact, each of you now feel yourself here, listening to a lecture on metaphysics. Now this actual and indubitable fact belongs to a thing, or a reality, which is called your life. What is this—your life, our lives, the life of each one of us? It would appear to be something without importance, for science has never busied itself with this. Nevertheless, that reality, so neglected scientifically, proves to have the formidable condition that it contains for each one of us all the rest of the realities, including the reality called science and the one called religion, in that science and religion are only two of the innumerable things that man creates in his own lifetime.

Before metaphysics begins to tell us what the universe is, is it not worth while to stop to survey this earlier and most humble but inescapable fact that metaphysics itself is only what man—you and I—create in our own lives, and that, consequently, this life is something earlier, something antecedent to, whatever metaphysics—or any other science, or religion itself—is going to discover for us?

I do not know whether or not what I call 'my life' is important, but it does seem that, important or not, it was here before all the rest, including before God Himself, for all the rest—including God—must be taken as given to us and as being—for me—within my own life.

What, then, is life? Do not search far afield; do not try to recall learned expressions of wisdom. The fundamental truths must be always at hand, for only thus are they fundamental. Those that one must go forth to seek are the ones that are found only in a single place—the particular, localized, provincial truths, the truths in a corner, not the basic ones. Life is what we are and what we do; it is, then, of all things the closest to each one of us. Put a hand on it and it will let itself be grasped like a tame bird.

If, on coming here a moment ago, someone had asked you where you were going, you would have said, 'We are going to hear a lecture on metaphysics'. And here you are, listening to me. The fact has no importance.

Nevertheless, it is what makes up your life. I am sorry for you, but truth obliges me to say that your life now consists of a thing of miniscule importance. But if we are sincere, we will recognize that the greater part of our existence is made up of similar insignificant affairs. We go, we come, we do this or that, we think, we love or we do not love, and so on. From time to time, our lives seem suddenly to take on tension, as if to rear up, to concentrate and become dense. It may be a great sorrow or a great desire that overcomes us; we say that things of great importance are happening to us. But note that in terms of our lives, this variety of emphasis, this experiencing or not experiencing something momentous, is a matter of indifference in that the frenetic and culminating hour is just as much a matter of life (and no more) as is the common business of our habitual moments.

The result, then, is that in this inquiry into life's pure essence, the first view we get of it appears to us as the sum of what we do, the sum of our activities which, so to speak, furnish it. *Life is what we do and what happens to us.*

Our method is going to consist in noting the attributes of our lives, one after another, in such order that from the most external we advance toward the most internal, from the periphery of living we narrow down toward its palpitating center. We will then find a successive series of definitions of life, each of which conserves and deepens the preceding ones.

And so the first definition we find is this: to live is what we do and what happens to us, from thinking or dreaming or worrying, to playing the market or winning battles. It is important to me that you recognize that this is not a joke, but a truth as platitudinous as it is basic and unquestionable. I intend to talk to you not of things that are abstruse and far away, but of your life itself, and I begin by saying that, at this moment, your life consists in listening to me. I am sure that you will resist this truth, but there is no alternative because this listening to me is what you are doing now, and it is what now makes up your life.

But life is always a 'now', and it consists of what 'now' is. The past and the future of your life have reality only in the now, and this is thanks to the fact that you now remember your past or anticipate your future. In this sense, life is pure actuality—it is punctual, a point in the present—which contains all our past and all our future. Therefore, I am able to affirm that our life is what we are doing now. Do not, however, hold me guilty. What fault is it of mine that you resolved to come here this afternoon and, therefore, to make your life consist of listening to me? Why did you come?

I am not going to answer this question immediately, but some day I would like to answer it, although very seriously, for if life is always what we are doing, it is very important to analyze *why* we are doing one thing, and not another. It is characteristic of doing that everything which is done is done for something and that, consequently, life lives always on a 'why?'; faithful to my promise to talk to you about your lives, I am obliged to make you note the obvious truth that this consists not only in listening to me, but in trying to find out *why* you are listening to me. Perhaps this may make some of you blush, because I know that not all of you have come for good reasons. Very well, next time you will take more care about what you do, that is to say, about how you live. The purpose of these lessons is no other than to incite each of you to take care of your life; for you have only one, and that one is composed of a given number—a very limited number—of instants, of nows, and to use that number badly is to destroy it, to kill a bit of your life. But we will talk further about this.

NOTHING of what we do would be our life if we did not take account of it. This is the first decisive attribute that we encounter; living is that strange, unique reality which has the privilege of existing for its own sake. All living is one's own living, feeling oneself live, knowing oneself to be existing, where knowing does not imply intellectual knowledge or any special wisdom but is that surprising *presence* which one's life has for every one of us. Without that knowing, without that awareness, an aching tooth would not hurt us.

The stone does not feel itself, nor does it know itself to be a stone. Toward itself, as toward everything else, it is totally blind. Living, on the other hand, is a revelation, a refusal to content oneself with being unless one sees or understands what one is, a becoming-acquainted with oneself. It is the incessant discovery that we make of ourselves and of the world around us. Now we come to the explanation and the juridical title of that strange possessive which we use when we say 'our life'; it is 'ours' because in addition to being our life, we take account of what it is, and of what it is exactly as it is. In perceiving ourselves and sensing ourselves, we take possession of ourselves, and this finding ourselves always in possession of ourselves, this perpetual and fundamental business of being present at what we do and are, differentiates living from everything else. The proud sciences, the sage wisdoms—these do no more than put to good use, particularize, and regiment this primary revelation of which life consists.

This seeing ourselves, this sensing ourselves, this presence of my life before me, which puts me in possession of it and makes it mine, is what the demented lack. The madman's life is not his own; strictly speaking, it is no longer life. Therefore, to see a madman is a most unsavory thing because he seems to have the complete semblance of a life; but this is only a mask behind which the genuine life is not there. Faced with the demented, we feel ourselves facing a mask, the essential and definitive mask. The madman, in not knowing himself, does not belong to himself; he has been expropriated, and expropriation, the passing into foreign possession, is what the old names of madness meant; we say deranged, alienated, removed, 'he is outside himself', he is 'gone', that is, gone from himself, he is 'possessed', that is, possessed by another. (Life is knowing oneself, it relies on evidence.)

In its very root and heart, living consists in knowing and understanding ourselves, in noticing ourselves and what surrounds us, in being transparent to ourselves. Therefore, when we posed the question 'What is our life?', we could clearly answer, gaily and without effort, 'Life is what we do', because life is knowing what we are doing; it is, in short, finding ourselves in the world and occupied with the things and the beings of the world.

This is not chiefly a matter of finding our bodies amid other corporeal things, and all of this within a great body or space that we would call the world. If there were only bodies, living would not exist; the bodies would roll against each other like billiard balls or atoms, some of them always on the outside, without any of them knowing each other or being important to each other. The world in which we find ourselves living is made up of things which are both agreeable and disagreeable, atrocious and benevolent, and favorable and dangerous; what is important is not that things may or may not be bodies, but that they touch us, interest us, caress us, threaten or torment us. Originally, what we call a body is only something that resists and impedes us, or sustains and carries us along; therefore, it is merely something favorable or something adverse. The world is, *sensu stricto*, that which affects us. And living is, for each one of us, finding himself in an ambit of subjects and matters that interest us. Thus, without knowing how, life finds itself at the moment when it discovers the world. There is no living except on a globe filled with other things, whether they be objects or creatures; it is seeing things and scenes, loving them or hating them, desiring them or fearing them. All living is a matter of busying oneself with the other person, the other thing, the other matter that is not oneself; all living is a living with, a finding oneself in the midst of a circum-stance,[2] a surrounding.

It follows that our life is not only our person, but that our world forms part of that life; it consists of the fact that the person is occupied by things or with them, and evidently what our life is depends as much on what our person is as on what our world is. Neither the one nor the other is closer to us; we do not first take account of ourselves and then of our surroundings, but living is, at root, a matter of finding ourselves confronting the world; with the world, within the world, submerged in its trafficking, its problems, the web of its misfortunes. But the opposite is also true; that world, being made up only of what affects each one of us, is inseparable from us. We are born with it, and world and person are vitally like those pairs of divinities of ancient Greece and Rome who were born together and lived together; the Heavenly Twins, for example, Castor and Pollux, the Dioscuri, pairs of gods who were frequently called *dii consentes*, the unanimous gods.

We live here, that is to say, we find ourselves on one spot in the world and it seems that we have come to this place of our own free will. Life does, in fact, leave a margin of possibilities within the world; but in this world, which is the world of now, we are not free to be or not to be. One can renounce life, but if one lives, one cannot choose the world in which one lives. This gives our existence a terribly dramatic aspect. Living is not entering by choice into a place previously chosen according to one's taste, as one picks a particular theater to go to

2. Ortega used the word circumstance as did sixteenth-century Englishmen, meaning 'that which stands around or surrounds' (OED); the current American meaning emphasizes pecuniary affairs. To indicate this difference, I have from time to time kept this key word in the translated text, written with a hyphen between the syllables, hoping that Ortega's meaning would leap to the reader's eye [*Translator's note*].

after dinner; living is finding oneself suddenly—and not knowing how—projected into, fallen into, submerged in a world that cannot be exchanged for any other, into the world of today. Our lives begin with the perpetual surprise of existing without any previous consent on our part, castaways on an unpremeditated globe. We did not give life to ourselves, but we met it at the very point where we met ourselves. We can compare our plight to that of a sleeper who is carried to the wings of a theater, and there, awakened with a push, is thrust down to the footlights and before the public. On finding himself there, what does this individual find? He finds himself caught accidentally in a difficult situation, without knowing how or why; somehow, he must, and with some decorum, resolve that sudden appearance before the public which he neither sought, prepared for, nor foresaw. Fundamentally, life is always unforeseen. Before entering on its stage, we have not been prepared or announced; yet that stage is always concrete and definite.

I think this image paints with some clarity the essence of living. Life is given to us—or better, it is thrown at us, or we are thrown into it—but the life we are given is a problem which we ourselves must resolve. And this is not only true of those cases of special difficulty which we describe as peculiarly filled with conflicts and afflictions, but of all cases. It is always like that. When you came here, you had to decide to live this space of time in this shape—you would bring yourselves here. Or, to put it another way, we live by upholding ourselves in mid-air, carrying the weight of our lives amid the corners of the world. And it does not matter whether our existence is gay or sad; whether it is one or the other, life is made up of an incessant effort to solve the problem posed by life itself.

If the bullet that the gun fires had a mind, it would feel that its trajectory was exactly predetermined by the powder and the firing point, and if we called this trajectory our life, the bullet would be simply a spectator in it, without intervening in it; the bullet neither fired itself, nor did it choose its target. But, by the same token, that way of existing cannot be called life. Life is never felt to be predetermined. However sure we are of what is going to happen to us tomorrow, we always see it as a possibility rather than as a certainty. This is another essential and dramatic attribute of our lives to be added to the previous ones. Just as our existence is at every moment a problem, big or small, which we must solve without being able to pass the solution over to someone else, so is it never a solved problem; from moment to moment, we find ourselves forced to choose between various possibilities. Is this not surprising? We have been flung into our lives and, at the same time, we must, on our own account, make what we have been flung into, we must fabricate it. Or, to put it another way, our life is our being. We are whatever it is, and nothing more. But that being is not predetermined, not resolved ahead of time; we must make its decisions ourselves, decide, for example, what we are going to be, decide what we are going to do when we leave here. This is what I call 'sustaining ourselves in mid-air, upholding our own being'. In it, there is neither rest or pause, because the dream, which is a form of biological living, does not exist for life in the basic sense in which we use this word. Dreaming, we do not live, except that upon waking and resuming life, we find it augmented by the fleeting memory of what we dreamed.

The elemental and established metaphors are as true as Newton's laws. In those venerable phrases which have become part of our language, on which we proceed at all hours as though on an island formed by what were coral insects, are encrusted perfect intuitions of the most basic phenomena. Thus, we frequently say that we suffer a 'heaviness', that we find ourselves in a 'grave' situation. Heaviness and gravity are taken over metaphorically from physical weight, from the weighing of a body on our own body, and weighing us down in the most intimate way. And, as a matter of fact, life always weighs on us, for it is made up of carrying itself, supporting itself, and leading itself forward. Yet nothing dulls the edge like habit, and ordinarily we forget that constant weight which we drag along and which, in truth, we are; but when faced with something unusual, we feel the weight all over again. While one heavenly body gravitates toward another and does not weigh on itself, a living body is, at once, both a weight that can be measured and a hand that upholds. Similarly, the word *alegría* (joy) comes perhaps from the word *aligerar*, which means to lighten, to make something lose weight. The man weighed down with worry goes to the tavern seeking *alegría;* he casts off his ballast, and the poor aerostat of his life goes gaily upward.

With all this, we have advanced notably in this vertical exploration, this descent into the deep being of our own lives. At our present level, living appears to us as a process of feeling ourselves forced to decide what we are going to be. Now we are no longer content, as we were earlier, with saying 'Life is what we do'; it is the combination of our occupations and the things of the world, because we have noted that all this doing and these occupations do not come to us automatically, mechanically imposed like a set of gramophone records, but are decided upon by us, and this being decided is their living quality; the execution of these decisions is, in large part, mechanical.

The great fundamental fact that I wanted to place before you is right here; we have just stated it. To live is to be continually deciding what we are going to be. Do you see the fabulous paradox that this holds? A being that consists not so much in what it is as in what it is going to be and, therefore, in that which is not yet. This essential and abysmal paradox is our life. This is not my fault.

There it is, in strict truth.

But perhaps some of you are now thinking, 'When does living begin to be what you say it is—deciding what we are going to be? We have been right here, listening to you for some time, without deciding anything, and yet— who can doubt it—we have certainly been living.'

To this I would answer as follows: 'Gentlemen, all this time you have been doing nothing but deciding again and again what you were going to be. Condemned to relative passivity as you are (in that you are listening), this is one of the less vital hours of your lives. Yet it coincides directly with my definition. Here is the proof. While you have been listening to me, some of you have perhaps wavered more than once between ceasing to pay attention to me (so as to go wandering among your own thoughts), or continuing generously to listen to what I have been saying. You decided on the one or the other— to pay attention or to allow yourselves to be distracted, to think about this subject or about something else; and this thinking about your life or about something else is what your life now is. And this is no less true of those who did not waver, but firmly stayed by their decision to hear me to the end. Moment after moment, you would have had to feel that resolution anew in order to continue being attentive. Even the firmest of our decisions must receive constant corroboration, must be always newly-charged like a gun in which the powder has not been used; in short, those decisions must be redecided. When you came in that door, you had decided that you were going to be listeners, and then you reiterated your intent many times; otherwise you would soon have escaped me.'

And now, this is enough so that we can extract its immediate consequences. If our life consists in deciding what we are going to be, this means that at the very root of our lives there is a temporal attribute; to decide what we are going to be is to decide on the future. And without stopping to examine them further, we now reap a whole fruitful harvest of discoveries. First, that our life is, most of all, a colliding with the future. The first thing we live is not the present or the past; no, it is the future. Life is an activity pointed toward the future; we find the present or the past afterward, in relation to that future [3].

3. The final paragraphs of this lesson repeat or rephrase the final ones of Lesson X of the course, *What Is Philosophy?* given in 1929. See *Obras Completas,* vol. VII [*Compilers' note*]. [Or see the English translation of the book of that name published by W. W. Norton & Company, 1961—*Translator's note*].

Lesson III

The difference between reparar (*to be conscious of*) *and*
contar con (*to rely on*). *Revision and correction of what
has been set forth. No one can leap away from his own life.
'To make a science' is something that happens in 'our lives'.
Life as biography. What is heaven? Evidence and truth.
Life brings us many obligations. Reflection: the two 'nows'.*

LAST TIME, I took you just where you were, and where
you now have come back to—listening to a lecture on
metaphysics. This is what you are doing now and it is
what now constitutes your life. Life is always a 'now',
and it consists of what 'now' is. Your life's past and your
life's future have their reality only in the 'now' and
thanks to the fact that you 'now' remember your past or
anticipate your future. In this sense, life is a single point
—the present—which contains all our past and all our
future. Therefore, I could assert that our life is what we
are doing *now*.

If we reflect on what we did in order to discover this,
we have the following: to be doing something is to be
attentive to what we are doing; in this case, we pay attention, you and I, to my words which are making a beginning in metaphysics. Benefiting from our attention, these
words stand in the foreground like the protagonists of
the matter; or, to put it another way, only of them do we
have a clear, emphatic, and definite consciousness. All the
rest we disregard.

But when we heard the words 'What is our life? What
is my life?', a change came over us. For a moment, we
ceased to pay attention to the words and tried to grasp at
their meanings. And, as there was talk of 'our' and 'mine',

46

our attention moved to seek out the person of each one of us concerned. Seeking, we found the person and made him the new protagonist; or, what is the same thing, in this new 'now' each of us is beginning to have a clear, definite, and emphatic consciousness of his own self. I have 'seen' my own self, as earlier I had heard specific words. Where I said 'I', each of you must put your own self. I saw my own self: 'seeing' here means that I took hold of myself, that I grasped myself with complete attention, that I had a full, complete, immediate, and distinct consciousness of myself as I am, just as I had previously become immediately and completely conscious of the words I was hearing.

Now, if I found myself, if I caught myself with full attention; if I grasped myself, where did I find myself? Where did I seek myself? Note that in due time, this is going to be very important. I found myself there where I already was: namely, in the immediately previous 'now', and that consisted in my paying attention to certain definite words. And as I became aware of myself in this new 'now', I surprised myself paying attention to those words. So I did nothing now but catch a glimpse of my previous situation.

But note that then I was paying attention not to my person but *only* to some words; *only* of them did I have a clear and separate consciousness. In that situation, I might say that *nothing* existed in the universe except the words to which I was attending. How is it that now, when I catch a glimpse of that situation, I find that, in addition to words, I myself was there? Because if you look well, you will note that on finding yourselves, you never had an impression of finding something new, but, rather, that it was strange to find something which had not been lost, something you already knew was there although not in the form of a clear and separate consciousness.

At the proper moment, this distinction will furnish us

with formidable bits of information. Once you note them, you will recognize that this is one of the most natural things in the world. In order to have a clear and separate consciousness of something, we must give it our full attention just as, in order to see a thing well, we must turn our eyes directly toward it. Attention takes one object out of a confused group of them and sets bounds to it, emphasizes everything about it, makes it conspicuous. And how can we do this, how can we turn our attention to something if we were previously not aware of it, if we paid it no heed, much less gave it special and conscious attention?

Therefore—and for whatever we say in this course, this is decisive—there are two ways of becoming aware of something, of having something exist for me: one in which I become aware of the thing as separate and distinct, in which (let us put it this way) I take it before me as man to man, make it a precise and limited end and purpose of my becoming aware; and the other way in which the thing exists for me without my reflecting on it.

Earlier, when I was carefully seeking precise words, I was not conscious of myself any more than of the bench or the armchair on which I sit; yet both I and the bench existed for me, were in some manner there in front of me. The proof of this is that if anyone had moved the bench, I would have noticed that something in my situation had changed, that something was not the same as it had been a minute before. This shows that in some way I was aware of the bench and its position, that in some manner I was *relying on* the bench. Similarly, when we go down the stairs we have no precise consciousness of each step, but we rely on all of them. And it is true that, in general, we have no precise consciousness of the greater part of the things that exist for us; yet we do depend on them.

The most extreme example of this is our own person. Ordinarily, there is nothing that man reflects on less than himself; yet there is also nothing that he depends on more continually than on his own self. I always exist for myself, but only from time to time have I a real consciousness of myself. And as consciousness is a term too packed with special tradition in the history of philosophy (and starting from what we have just finished saying, I propose to rectify this at the proper time—a rectification which will allow us to do no less than try to move beyond the whole of modern idealism), let us put this discovery which we have just made into two new technical terms—*reparar*, which is the same as what was traditionally called 'being conscious of something', and the simple *contar con* (count on, rely on, depend on), which expresses that effective presence, that existing for myself, which all the ingredients of my situation always possess.

Now we can put this into a clear statement: earlier, I had no consciousness of myself, I was not watching myself, but I did depend on my self. Therefore, on seeking myself in the earlier 'now', it was possible for me to find that I was already there, that I already existed for myself, and that, thanks to this, I could catch myself, emphasize myself, reflect on myself; in short, I could have a clear and separate consciousness of my self.

We will now see how this happens with all the components of what I call life; when we face them and define them, they appear with an air of obvious truth, an air of 'things we already know'—that is to say, an air of things that were already there in front of us, existing for us— and our definition will do no more than discover for us certain intimate and customary friends whom we have always had without really knowing it until now. It is possible that in the previous talk, hearing some of my statements about life, you may have said, 'Man, it's true! I never thought of that!', which is what we usually say when someone brings us to a sharp recognition of something that we had relied on and taken for granted. All the evident truths have this characteristic—that when we discover them for the first time, it seems to us that we have always known them, but had not noticed them; there they were before us, but veiled and covered. Therefore, it is true that truth is discovered; perhaps truth is no more than discovery, the lifting of a veil or a cover from what was already there and on which we were already counting.

Having said this, let us go back to the paragraphs in which I was discovering the first attribute or characteristic which we found as distinctive of our lives:—'Living is what we do and what happens to us, from thinking or dreaming or worrying to playing the market or winning battles. . . .' But of course nothing we do would be our lives if we did not take account of it. 'This is the first decisive attribute that we encounter; living is that strange, unique reality which has the privilege of existing for its own sake. All living is one's own living, feeling oneself alive, knowing oneself to be existing, where knowing does not imply intellectual knowledge or any special wisdom, but is that surprising *presence* which one's life has for every one of us. Without that knowing, without that awareness, an aching tooth would not hurt us.

'The stone does not feel itself, nor does it know itself to be a stone. Toward itself, as toward everything else, it is totally blind. Living, on the other hand, is a revelation, a refusal to content oneself with being unless one sees or understands what one is, a becoming-acquainted with oneself. It is the incessant discovery that we make of ourselves and of the world around us. . . . In perceiving ourselves and sensing ourselves, we take possesssion of ourselves, and this finding ourselves in possession of ourselves, this perpetual and fundamental business of being present at what we do and are, differentiates living from everything else. The proud sciences, the sage wisdoms— these do no more than put to good use, particularize, and regiment this primary revelation of which life consists.

'This seeing ourselves, this sensing ourselves, this pres-

ence of my life before me, which puts me in possession
of it, which makes it mine, is what the demented lack'.

In its deepest and most secret roots, living consists in
knowing ourselves and comprehending ourselves, in being aware of ourselves and of what surrounds us, in a
form of being that to itself is transparent. Therefore,
when we began the question 'What is our life?', we could
answer gaily and without effort, 'Life is what we do—of
course—because living is knowing what we do; it is, in
short, finding oneself in the world and occupied with the
things and the beings of the world'.

In short, I ended, my life is evident, by which I meant
to say that everything in it and whatever forms part of it
exists for me and is transparent to me. What happens in
the cells of my body is not transparent to me; it does not
exist for me as part of my life, nor do the things that
happen in the psychic mechanism of what I call my soul.
More than this, body and soul do not exist for me; vitally, they do not form part of my life. Body and soul are
two intellectual constructions of mine, two hypotheses,
two theories which I have made or have received from
others in order to clarify for myself certain problems
which my life possesses for me. What exists vitally for
me, then, are my theory of the cells and my theory about
the soul; that is to say, these are two convictions of mine,
but the cells themselves and the soul itself do not form
part of my life. The savage neither has nor can have the
idea of body or the idea of soul; yet, nevertheless, he
lives.

But let us go back to the earlier section which I am re-
peating. In this description which I am making of that
phenomenon, that fact which I call 'my life', the life of
each of you, I must, for reasons you will see in due
course, begin with formulae which only in a first approximation are sure and certain. I must make use of words
of which many already have a more or less technical
meaning; this is precisely what we are going to rectify,

and sometimes fundamentally. So here it is: I needed to express to you the fact that an essential characteristic or attribute constituent in my life and in everything in it is what exists for me and is manifest to me. The clearest and most obvious expression is to say that to live is to know oneself to be alive, to know oneself existing, to be well aware of what I am and what the other things that surround me are. But to know, to be conscious of, something is a special and more or less intellectual way of being aware. Therefore, I added immediately to those terms this correction—'where "knowing" does not imply any intellectual knowledge or special wisdom, but deals with that surprising presence which one's own life has for each and every one of us; without *that* kind of knowing oneself, without that manner of taking account, not even an aching tooth would hurt us'.

These statements, in a first approximation which makes a progressive comprehension of the matter easier for you, now impel me to go back over them in order to correct them, to polish them, and to substitute for them other statements in a second approximation, and so on. This we will do with all the others. Thus, today we have sharpened and clarified the expression of that first characteristic of life, which is knowing oneself, being evident to oneself. Now, we note that there was an error in those words. When my teeth ache, the fact that they ache is not a form of knowing; knowing is not an ache, but, undoubtedly, the fact of an ache implies an ingredient which is the existence of this ache for me, the taking account of it in the sense of having to recognize it. In addition to this simple and primary taking account of the matter, without which the ache would not hurt me, I can be specially aware of it, can have a full, clear, and separate consciousness of it, in short, can know it *sensu stricto*.

But this knowing is not the simple aching, just as my relying on the bench on which I sit is not a special awareness of it. What is true is this: as my life with whatever forms a part of it is here, present before me, as it exists in the peculiar primary form of my relying on it, depending on it, *it is always possible in principle* that I may reflect on it, may lift it into full and clear consciousness, into effective knowing. In this sense, but only in this sense, is my statement valid: life is evident, that is, potentially. Speaking more precisely, we could say, my life is preconscious, or is preknown to me. I rely on it in such a form that it is always possible to convert this 'counting on' into an effective 'being conscious of', into effective evidence. In the same way, we could say that life is preconscious, or that it is preknown. Therefore, an effective knowing of it is a 'stumbling on it', a meeting with what we already had but had under cover.

With this, we close the corrective parenthesis. So that your notes may be orderly, I suggest that you head what you have been hearing with this phrase:—'Clarification in a second approximation of the phrase: life is evident, it is knowing itself, being fully aware of itself'.

Of course, this correction, this clarification, is by no means the only one that I shall have to make on this subject. On the contrary, this is a fundamental subject which, at some opportune moment, will occupy us *au fond* and in great detail. But I needed to make that clarification now so that you would not misunderstand what I am going on to say.

As for the rest, remember what our present task is. I began a course in metaphysics, and the first thing that occurred to me to say was that metaphysics is something that man makes; making it consists of seeking a basic orientation of his situation. This assumes that man's situation is one of basic *dis*orientation. But the fact is that you are not here, studying metaphysics, because you are disoriented but, on the contrary, because you are extremely well-oriented. You know many things; you know what the physical and the social world are, and, because you know this, you decided to study a career, and not just any career, but this particular one which you chose for many and very definite reasons. The fact that you are here is a result of the fact that you are well-oriented.

Well then, instead of asking you to enter into my situation—which is what is implied in that definition of metaphysics—I am going to do as I always have done—just the opposite. I will go to you; I will take you in your situation. I am starting with the indubitable fact that you are here, doing what you are doing, namely, attending a course in metaphysics.

Now, that fact pertains to a reality which is the closest one to every one of you, that reality which each of you calls his life and with which science has never busied itself; on the contrary, it has seemed to give this no importance, to take it for granted, leaving it unattended and leaping over it *a la torera*. Yet this trivial reality, life, our life, in the commonest sense of the term, undoubtedly possesses the formidable characteristic that all the other realities, whatever they may be, are included within it because all of them exist for us in the measure in which we live, that is, in the measure in which they appear in our lives. Just as no one, to quote an Arabian saying, can leap away from his shadow, so no one can leap away from his life, and, therefore, everything with which we have contact, everything that pretends to exist for us, must somehow present itself within our own lives.

Nevertheless, without giving the matter undue importance—at least for the moment—it seems natural that we should clarify this most ordinary reality which we commonly call 'our life', 'my life', especially now that it includes the fact that you are before me here and now and that I am, here and now, in front of you. And our present task has no other pretension than to describe with great exactness what it is that makes up our life such and as it presents itself. We have not yet made any doctrinal, formal, scientific affirmation about the importance which that reality may have in the system of the universe. Let us say, then, that we are in the antechamber of the science of metaphysics in that if we busy ourselves with 'our lives', it is because we stumbled against them as we were about to enter the arcane interior of metaphysics; that is to say, we found life in the antechamber, set ahead of science, since on going to make a science, which is our indisputable situation today, we found that this 'going to make a science' is something that is happening to us in 'our lives'.

The assumption—so that you may understand me—is, as I told you, that on answering the question 'What is my life?', you do not seek the reply in this science or that, in what, for better or worse, you know of them, but that you fasten your attention on the common meaning which the word 'life' has when each human being—the sage as well as the peasant or the savage—talks of his life and says that things in it are going well or bad for him, in short, of life in the biographic sense of the term.

If I ask 'What is heaven?', it is almost certain that you will start to reply with answers taken from astronomy, not noting that, for the moment, the question should be answered according to its most immediate and common meaning; namely, that heaven is what I see at night, therefore, what I see on high, as and how I see it, and nothing more. The astronomer can add many other things, but, for the moment, heaven means to him exactly the same thing that it does to the peasant who goes back to the village at night with his mule, under the twinkling stars, singing as he goes.

I am not, then, creating a theory *about* our life, but I am describing it in the same fashion as I might describe this wall. I speak, therefore, of something for which you have as much data as I could have—inasmuch as I am talking about the lives of every one of you! My mission, for now, is only to make you become aware of the essential components of your lives, of the principal ingredients which make up its structure. If I were describing this wall, you would keep your eyes fixed on it in order to see whether the wall and whatever was happening to it was what my description said; this you should now do with the facts of your life—to see whether the same theory that is being talked about and is here in front of us fulfils just what our words are saying about it, this is what is called evidence. And when something has been said that is evident in that sense, one has uttered an absolute truth.

You, then, are the ones who must, with your own vision, judge whether what I am saying about our lives is evident or not or—which is the same thing—is the truth.

Today, we have, in a longitudinal sense, gone no further than we went earlier. On the contrary, we have taken a step backward in order to make sure of those first characteristics that our lives present when we direct our attention toward them. We have made specific their first attribute—life as becoming thoroughly aware of itself. According to this, whatever forms part of my life does so *because* I become thoroughly aware of it and only insofar as I do this. This becoming aware is not a matter of consciousness, of reflecting upon, or of knowing it, but it is the elemental observing, which we are going to call 'counting on'.

I have indicated briefly what method you ought to follow in order to understand and to test what I am saying. This method is evidence, and it consists in finding out whether there is, in the thing talked about, exactly what is said about it.

In the next lesson, we will do with the second attribute of our lives the same thing we have done with the first. This second attribute I expressed by saying that life is circumstantial, concerned with what surrounds one; to live is to find myself, like it or not, handed over to what is about me. This attribute is dramatic. But the third one is much more so; it goes this way—life is decision.

If life consisted solely of its first attribute and was no more than a becoming completely aware of, a taking account of—as the entire modern period believed—living would be the same as being present at a spectacle, whether comic, tragic, or gay; one would be only a spectator. But as life is also circumstantial, a matter of surroundings, with man being—whether he likes it or not—involved in a definite social ambience, we will find life to be a taking account of, a becoming aware of the fact that I am submerged in those surroundings, a castaway in an element strange to me, where I have no choice but to be constantly doing something in order to sustain myself in it, to keep myself afloat. I did not give life to myself; on the contrary, I find myself in the midst of it without desiring it, without having been consulted about it, without anyone asking my leave. But what was given to me without consulting me—my life—was not given to me ready-made. When I was given life, what was given to me was the inexorable necessity of having to do something on pain of ceasing to live if I refused; but not even this, because ceasing to live is also doing something, it is killing myself, regardless of the weapon—whether it be a rifle, or merely inanition.

Life, then, whether you like it or not, is always a matter of having to do something. The life that was given to me results in my having to make it for myself. It is given to me but not ready-made, as existence is given to the star or the stone, already fixed and without problems. What is given to me with life is occupation—the need to do things, a task, an obligation. Life gives many occupations, and the fundamental thing about these tasks is the need to decide, moment by moment, what we are going to do the next moment. Hence, I say that life is a matter of deciding, is decision.

So we have these three characteristics: first, life is awareness of itself; second, life makes itself; third, life decides itself.

But if, whether I like it or not, I must decide what I am going to do—in that no one can give me the decision ready-made—this means that life at every moment is bringing me face to face with various possibilities of doing. On leaving here, I *am able* to do many different things, and at least they are varied. Among them I must decide. The fact that I have to decide for myself implies that I am never decided in advance, as is the star whose orbit is fixed. Before deciding, then, I am undecided, perplexed. Here is a fourth attribute of life: life is . . . perplexity, continual and essential perplexity, and so forth and so on, because with all this, we have done no more than to begin the description of our life. In the next lesson, we will go on to analyze these characteristics a bit more minutely, as we did with the first one.

But in order not to lose time, note that we will start by going back for a moment to the beginning of this lesson, when, saying that our life is what we are now doing, I added, 'And how did we find out? Very simply', I went on, "because when, in a new "now", we framed the question "What is our life, my life?", we hastened to go back to the earlier "now" and there we saw it, caught it, found it.' In the first 'now', our activity consisted in paying attention to certain words. In this second 'now', what we are doing is thinking about ourselves, reflecting on the fact that we were previously doing that earlier thing. This new activity is called reflecting on or becoming conscious of ourselves. On seeking 'my life', I found myself in this room, listening to certain words; I took account of that. But the 'that' of which I took account— the 'finding myself listening in this room'—includes many things, or at least three: first, that I found myself, my 'I'; second, that I found that this 'I' was in a room; third, that I found that in the room I was doing something, that at least I was paying attention to certain words.

Lesson IV

The three elements of the encounter. Meeting the 'I'. Meeting the circumstances, the surroundings; temporal and social characteristics of the circumstance. The way of being there in the circumstance. Homogeneous and heterogeneous being there. To live is for me to exist outside myself. Parenthesis on the semantics of existing: active and effective being. New analysis of 'being there'. The immaterial character of circumstance.

LET US BEGIN by going back to the last moment of the previous lecture when, saying that our life is what we are doing now, I added 'And how did we find this out? Very simply, I went on, because when, in a new "now", we framed the question, "What is our life, my life?", we hastened to go back to the earlier "now" and there we saw it, caught it, found it. In the first "now", our activity consisted in paying attention to certain words. In this second "now", what we are doing is thinking about ourselves, reflecting on the fact that we were previously doing that earlier thing. This new activity is called reflecting on or becoming conscious of ourselves. Upon seeking "my life", I found myself in this room, listening to certain words; I took account of that. But the "that" of which I took account—the "finding myself listening in this room"—includes many things, or at least three: first, that I found myself, my "I"; second, that I found that this "I" was in a room; third, that I found that in the room, I was doing something, that at least I was paying attention to certain words.'

Let us now take these things that I found, one by one, and say about each one what, for the moment, is strictly

59

necessary.

First, I meet what I call 'I'. Who or what this 'I' is cannot, at the moment, offer us any urgent problem. This 'I' that I meet here is the same that I am continually talking about since it is the 'I' of my own life—in the commonest sense of the word. If this 'I' involves serious problems, they are not in question at the moment. It is enough for us that the meaning of that word has the same degree of precision, or imprecision, that it has when we use it in conversation, at home, in talking with a friend, or in writing in our private diaries.

Let us now go on to the second discovery: this consists of the fact that when I find myself, this 'I', I find it in a room. This, in spite of being highly trivial—or because of it—is more serious. The result is that on finding myself, I find not only this self, but I also find a room, that is, another thing which is not 'I'. And, moreover, not only do I find myself as an individual thing and also (and separate) find the room, but I find myself *in* the room, within it and, therefore, not apart from it, but quite the opposite. It may be said that this is accidental. I remember that a moment ago I was in the street. Precisely; that I find myself in the room or in the street may be an accident, but it is not accidental that when I find myself, I always find myself within something else; this, I can be certain, will be something other than the 'I'.

This is the serious thing that I mentioned earlier. When man encounters himself, he does not do this in and by himself, apart and alone; on the contrary, he always finds himself within another thing which, in turn, is made up of many other things. He finds himself surrounded by what is not himself, by a surrounding, by a circumstance, by a landscape. In the vital idiom of our most common life, we usually, and in general, call this circumstance the world. Let us say, then, that always when I meet myself, I find that self in the world; but again, one must be careful not to give this term 'world' any learned meaning, but hold to the commonest one: 'world' means everything about me, everything that surrounds me. This means that on finding myself, I find myself a prisoner.

This makes us aware of a small error that we committed when we said that it was in reflecting on my life that I first encountered myself. If I found myself in a room or, in general, anywhere in the world, my observation would first have had to deal with the room, then with the world, and only after considering that world would I come upon myself. First, one encounters the prison, then the prisoner within it. Let us not be too formal with this 'first' and that 'then' but leave this fact as noted. In living, I am always occupied with the things —material or personal—that surround me; I pay heed to the circum-stance, the surroundings, and in order to find myself, I suspend that normal attention to what lies about me and seek myself in it, hunt for myself among things, disregarding them, and focusing on myself. This discovery that a *consciousness* of myself comes essentially, and not by accident, after my *consciousness* of the world is very important; in other words, I am aware of myself only when I cease to pay attention to the world, when, in terms of attention, I retreat or retire from the world. Certainly, this pulling back from the world is never effective; at times, we would like to retire from it, and we struggle to accomplish this in part, or in approximation; not only do we fail to achieve it but, even when we pretend to succeed, it costs a tremendous effort at abstraction (to keep ourselves apart from the world).

This emphasizes the fact that our life, in itself, consists in our being consigned to the world; and life is always a matter of *counting on* ourselves and *counting on* the world, simultaneously and inseparably, giving no priority to either one. Only when it is a matter of awareness, of being conscious of the one or the other, do 'before' and 'after' enter.

Within the enormous surrounding territory (circumstance) which is this world, we can move about with a certain freedom; we come and go, travel and emigrate, but we cannot escape from its complete and inexorable circumference. Hence, we told you that 'Life . . . leaves a margin of possibilities within the world; but in this world, which is the world of now, we are not free to be or not to be. One can renounce life, but if one lives, one cannot choose the world in which one lives. This gives our existence a terribly dramatic aspect. Living is not entering by choice into a place previously chosen according to one's taste, as one picks a theater to go to after dinner; living is finding oneself suddenly—and not knowing how—projected into . . . a world that cannot be exchanged for any other, into the world of today. Our lives begin with the perpetual surprise of existing without any previous consent on our part, as castaways on an unpremeditated globe.'

The world of our lives is not only circumstance, that which lies about us in a spatial sense (we will see later whether this expression is really adequate), but is also something which is completely analogous to what the theory of relativity says about the world of physics. The circumstance of space is conditioned by the circumstance of time. This bit of earth differs according to the period in which we come to it. Twenty centuries ago, these square meters of terrain we now occupy held no university hall but probably a forest of oak trees. Moreover, the surroundings are not composed solely of things in the strict sense of the term but also of people. One's surroundings are also made up of human society; the world is also a 'world' in the human sense. One lives in the university world, or the working world, or the world of the elegants.

This, for the moment, is sufficient amplification of the second point, which went like this: I found that I was *in* a room.

When you leave here, you can say that you have come

from a lecture on metaphysics in which all they did was to tell you that you were in a room. Is it possible that a serious discipline would take the trouble to emphasize so formidable piece of the obvious, so frightful a commonplace? Nevertheless, please note that merely by focusing a bit of attention on what we were saying when we said that we found ourself *in* a room, we began to discover certain serious matters. And this without really doing more than taking account of what we were saying. We did not add anything, but we took possession a bit more firmly of what we were thinking when we said that. When we use those words currently, we do not think out all that they say; that is, we do not fully think through our own thought, but we use this mechanically, without realizing its entire content. Since any thought of ours and, in general, our acts can be exercised in two ways—one fully and completely, the other only partially —this is a matter that in the course of our study must interest us very much.

But we did not limit ourselves solely to thinking in full of what we ordinarily think only in part; strictly speaking, what I said about my 'being in a room' is only a minute fraction of what could and should be said. Nevertheless, I repeat, to load the phrase with our attention was enough to force from it an important drop of juice.

At that, we became conscious only of part of the phrase—first of the word 'I'; second, in the phrase 'in a room', we focused only on the word 'in'. But there is another word that escaped us, and it now deserves attention. It seems an inoffensive word, and almost insignificant—the verb 'to be'.

'I *am* in a room.' Something was revealed to us about this when we said in reference to the relationship of the 'I', that I am with the room, that it is a relationship which consists of nothing less than the fact that in man's inexorable condition, being unable to escape his surroundings, he is confined to the world.

What does it mean—that I *am* in a room? What is this about *being* there?

The table *is* in the room; that is to say, the big piece of matter which is the table forms part of the greater piece of matter which is this room. In this case, 'is' means to form part of a whole. If we take the table away, the empty space it leaves will have to be filled with another unit of the same size as the table, with another bulk of extensive matter, even though this be only air or ether. Between the room and the table there is homogeneity.

But when I say that *I am* in the building, does this mean I form part of it? This might be true of my body; but I am not my body, or at least I am not solely my body. What the devil! I, this I, of which I am accustomed to talk during my lifetime, the I that lives my life, this is something unique, not to be confused with anything else, and heterogeneous to everything! I am not only a piece of matter; but this does not mean that I think I am made up of something immaterial—whether you call it soul, spirit, or what you will. It is not because of this. Perhaps I think that you, too, are made up of something immaterial, that you, too, have a soul or a spirit; nevertheless, I am not to be confused with you and am basically heterogeneous to you. What the devil! I am nothing other than myself; I am unique; there is no other that could be myself, not even another I! Did any one of you, however much he may be 'another I', suffer the toothache which *I* had to endure yesterday afternoon? Does anyone else among you put forth for me the effort that I am putting forth in an attempt to understand this professor of metaphysics who is talking across the table from me? This other person may put forth an effort that is completely equal to mine, but the effort which I put forth he does not exert; nor can he. He puts forth his, and I put forth mine. I am, then, heterogeneous to every other 'I', however much of an 'I' it may be.

Well now—and for today, let me suggest it merely in passing—please note the huge philosophic sin that we have committed. 'Homogeneous' means of the same genus, that which is thought with the same concept. Heterogeneous means that which is thought with another concept. 'I' is the same concept whether applied to me or applied to any of you. Nevertheless, here we come up against the indestructible evidence that in this case, homogeneity of concept implies heterogeneity of being. But this tremendous paradox must not detain us now. We will meet it face to face when occasion arises. What is interesting now is that you recognize the fact that the 'I' of every one of you is unique. It is simply the 'I' that lives your life, and that life which it lives is lived by no one else, *even though all the contents of both lives might be equal.*

Now you understand why I said, 'I am not only a piece of matter; but this does not mean I think that I am made up of something immaterial—whether you call it soul, or spirit'. What makes me not a piece of matter is not especially that the piece of matter is a piece of matter, whereas I, on the contrary, am immaterial, but something far more fundamental and decisive; namely, that I am no other than I, that I am unique, whereas all the rest, whether matter or another spirit, is another thing, something other than I.

The decisive element, then, in the meaning of the words 'I am in a room' is that in this case, he who is in the room is basically something other than the room, heterogeneous to it, and that this 'being in it' is not the same as forming a part of it.

But what, then, is this 'being' which seemed inoffensive, almost insignificant? It is enough to transpose into a positive phrase what we have just put in negative form: my being in the room is a matter of my existing in something other than myself; therefore, it is existing outside of myself, in strange territory; it is being constitutionally a stranger, in that I do not form a part of that in which I am, I do not have anything to do with it.

And as we said that this—being amid surroundings or in a world—is a constituent part of my life, this means that man exists outside himself, in another, a foreign country—who knows if it is an enemy country?—not at different periods and from time to time, but essentially and always. Man is essentially a stranger, an emigrant, an exile.

But this statement—to live is for me to exist outside myself—obliges us to undertake an operation exactly opposite to the one we had to perform on the expression 'life is evident'. Then we had to correct that one because it was true only for a first approximation. Now we meet the opposite situation. The statement—to live is to exist outside myself—is . . . all too true. This is because the early use of it has—along with some didactic advantages which justify my hurrying to employ it—the disadvantage that you cannot yet understand it in its full and precise meaning.

In fact, there is used in it the word 'exist', although the meaning of that word is not yet clear to you. First, let us clarify that meaning, but putting it in parentheses, outside the analysis of life that we are making, so you do not grow confused.

We say that this table and this light exist, and, for the moment, we do not suggest more than this; we mean only that there is such a thing. The merchant, for instance, will tell us that in his shop he has many 'existences' of a certain article, that is, that this article comes in a great many examples.

On the other hand, we say of the unicorn and the centaur that they do not exist, that is, that there is no such thing. We could, like the merchant, say that of the centaur and the unicorn we have no 'existences'.

I repeat, then, that for the moment we understand the existing or not existing of a thing simply to mean that

there is such a thing or there is not. Now, the fact that
there is something does not say anything about it except
that I can or I must meet it in a certain ambit. Let us not
go into detail about the matter but move directly to what
concerns us. The ambit where I can or must encounter
what I call existent, in the commonest sense of the word,
is not just any ambit. For example, in the ambit of
poetry, the centaur goes galloping with the stolen maiden
flung across his shoulders; in that ambit, therefore, there
are, there exist, other centaurs. On the other hand, we
say that there are none of them in the world because by
the term 'world' we apparently understand the ambit of
existent things in a special sense. The geometrician asks
himself if a definite, specific figure exists; the mathematician asks himself if a specific number exists—for example,
if there is an infinite number, the number greater than all
other numbers. Each of these has reference to a certain
type of existence: the purely mathematical, the ideal ambit of pure mathematical objects. In contemporary mathematics, a theorem of existence is used which determines
just that—whether there is or is not this number or that
one.

Therefore, existence and existing in the sense of 'there
being something' do no more than transfer us to a circumference whose characteristic is decisive for what
those words come to mean.

But, nevertheless, it cannot be denied that even in
common language 'to exist' has a principal meaning
which, in a certain way, excludes the others. For something to exist is not, in this primordial sense, simply that
there is such a thing, but that there is this thing in the
ambit of effective 'real things'. But—and the fact is curious—we note that we lack words adequate to express in
our own thought the basic difference in the way of being
between centaurs and horses. In principle, we could imagine all the elements of the centaur, everything the centaur is, with the same precision that we use in describing

the horse. Nevertheless, the centaur that exists in poetry
is not there, not effectively there as is the horse in real
life. But the centaur is not alone in this; in respect to the
species 'horse', in the broad sense of the term, there are
also horses which, one must say, strictly speaking, do not
exist. For example, there is Rosinante in *Don Quixote* but
not in reality. Here, the thing that there is and the thing
that there is not are the same; they vary only in the sense
of existing.

This makes us realize that in talking of the existence of
something, we must distinguish between two things, the
thing that exists, and the existing of this thing—or, in
other words, *what* there is, and the being that is in the
what. This 'what', that 'something', mean the mere essence, the group of ingredients which make up a thing; in
short, what a thing is. The centaur and the horse each has
its essence, the one neither more nor less than the other.
But the centaur does not make its essence effective, it is
not effectively what it is; the centaur is ineffectively
itself—it does not exist. The essence remains without
being put in force. Well then, in its primary and strict
sense, the existence of something means the execution or
achievement of that something. In place of using our
word 'existence', Aristotle said, 'taken as work, accom-
plished'—*enérgeia on*—and the Scholastics translated
that term saying, 'put into action', to be in force, in actuality.

If we say that the whiteness of this wall exists, we
mean to say that the essence of this whiteness is achieved;
we would say that the white whitens, that it achieves its
whiteness. On the other hand, the whiteness of Leda's
swan did not effect its whiteness, did not achieve execution. When thinking of the myth, I think not only of the
whiteness, but also that the whiteness was achieved. But
to think of the achievement of something is not the same
as achieving it.

Existence, then, means, *sensu stricto*, to be effectively,

actively, what one is; in short, it is the bringing into force of an essence.

If we now compare the meaning of existence as execution, achievement, with the meaning of existence as 'there being something', we will note that in this second case, when we say of something that it exists, that it is there, we do not, strictly speaking, say anything about the something, but about ourselves. Therefore, on saying 'there is a thing' we understand that we can or we must find it within a certain compass. Of the thing itself, we say nothing; we say only what happens to us concerning it, namely, that we can or we must encounter it. But this implies no effort from the thing. Because the finding of it is a matter that happens to us, nothing happens to the thing.

But in the strict meaning of existing as the becoming effective of a thing, an essence, something does happen to the thing; it continues to be effectively what it is, to be 'making its essence'. This concept of existence is taken from the point of view of the thing (and expresses the sensation that the thing would have were it capable of feeling, the sensation of the effort it was exerting in order to make its essence effective, *to be itself*), meanwhile, the other meaning—existing simply in the sense of 'there is something'—is a concept from the point of view of the spectator who sees, who finds the thing from outside it.

There you have the abstruse considerations to which we have been brought simply by the effort to clarify the meaning of the verb 'to exist'. There was reason to judge that the statement 'to live is to exist outside oneself' was too exact, although I used it deliberately and was fully aware of its dangers. But now that we have achieved a certain clarity about the meaning of 'to exist', let us make the most of our work by examining the consequences which that clarity holds for our phrase, 'to live is for me to exist outside myself'. In place of 'to exist', let us say 'to achieve my essence'. Then we will have this—'to live is to work out my essence, or what I am, outside of myself'; outside of myself means outside of my essence, in what is not my essence, in an element strange to my being.

The element in which this table works out its being, effects its essence, is not heterogeneous, not alien to it. The place *in which* the table acts out its being, executes it, is not heterogeneous to it. Its essence is a combination of atoms; its surroundings—this room, the planet, and so on—is also composed of atoms. But, in addition, the essence of this combination of atoms which is the table includes all the rest of the cosmic atoms and vice versa; the others would not be *what they are* without those and vice versa. Strictly speaking, then, the essence of the table is the same as that of its surroundings. For the table to exist will not be a matter of achieving its being outside itself in that what is outside it is the same as what is inside it.

But the matter of our life is the opposite of this. I am unique; my essence is mine alone and must achieve itself in something else. Here, then, existing does not coincide with the essence, with one's own being.

Our case would be rather like that of an actor who plays Hamlet. The essence of Hamlet must be brought to life in a theater; it must exist *in* a theater. Hamlet must emerge from himself in order to be activated by an actor on a specific stage; that is, Hamlet must be made to live by something that is not Hamlet. So it is with our life. I must achieve myself in the world, among things, among other men, with a body which has fallen to me by chance and which suffers illnesses, with a soul that perhaps is not very well endowed with will or memory or intelligence.

Here you can close that parenthesis which we might entitle 'Semantics of the term "to exist"'.

ALTHOUGH MUCH of what we have been saying will serve us well in the future, let us recognize that between this and that humble 'being in a room' is interposed so great a distance that we do not see a way open from one to the other. We do not see how our being in this room is achieving our essence. For the moment, this phrase remains irremediably distant, without evidence, abtruse.

Therefore, we must go back to the more trivial, must return to the analysis of the verb 'to be' which we abandoned for that other, more learned, and much more abstract term, 'to exist'.

We were saying that my being in a room does not mean that I am part of it, because the room and, in general, the surroundings, the world, are all completely heterogeneous to me. The surroundings are something other than me, and my being in them is equivalent to my being outside myself, in a strange element. But this is precisely what it is now useful for us to understand clearly and in its concrete content.

If I say that for me to be in the room is to be outside myself, I have expressed my relationship with this room by means of a term of space, 'outside of'. But it is evident that this space term can have here only a metaphorical meaning. Strictly speaking, only a point in space and the material ascribed to it can be outside of another thing. Space consists precisely in the possibility that some things may be outside other things. Space is the coexistence of points some of which are together and outside of other points.

Well now, in the first place, I am not a point in space; therefore, I cannot be outside the other points in space. Second, the expression which was formulated was not that I would be outside the other things but that my being in the room was equivalent to my being outside myself. The point of space is not nor can it be outside itself; for the very reason that each one is in itself does it manage to be outside the others.

Therefore, the phrase 'being outside oneself', interpreted in terms of space, seems absurd and can hope to be intelligible only if it is understood as a metaphor. To be 'outside' here means, in effect, no more than 'to be in the other'. That is to say, when we seek a concrete meaning for 'I myself being in the room' we fall back on the abstract expression.

The difficulty we meet in going forward arises from an error which, until this course of lectures is far advanced, we will commit again and again however careful may be my recommendations for avoiding it. This error impedes —and will impede for a long time—our descriptions of life. It consists of the fact that what we are describing —our life—is the most elemental thing, antecedent to all the rest, especially to science, since science is only one thing among the innumerable things that make up our life. And instead of devoting ourselves to what this elemental and primary reality is and to the face which its ingredients present in it, we put into the description of life that which is not life, but our wisdom about what there is in it. Physics, for example, makes us know that what surrounds us is space full of matter, which is made up of atoms that vibrate. Let us assume, for the moment, that this opinion of the physicists is absolutely true, that it is, therefore, a definitive opinion. (This supposition is very generous, for you are not unaware that in physics there is nothing definitive, nor can there be. But let us start with this in order to broaden the argument.) Well then, even in such a case, the result would always be that that opinion of the physicists would be no more than one of our opinions about what surrounds us in the world in which we live. But an opinion, a theory about our surroundings, however certain it may be, is not the same as our surroundings. On the contrary, it is a supposition about what our surroundings are, what they were before our theory, and what they will continue to be while our theory lasts and after it. My vital compass is not made up of atoms; even if it were, I would never need to do physics or to learn physics, but in the simple process of living I would encounter atoms without any need to think *about* my surroundings in order to discover them.

In analyzing the phrase 'I, being in a room', we will not manage to clarify the meaning of 'being' for the simple reason that in making for ourselves a problem of the 'I', of 'in', and of 'being', we have left 'room' as a thing clear in itself. And this neglect has given rise to our understanding in terms of learning, rather than of life, of what this ingredient is in my life now. We have understood 'room', being a thing held together by nails, to mean a physical body, a material space. And out of this have come all the difficulties, all the misfortunes through which we are passing. It was inevitable that if the room were a material space, then the 'I, being in it' would also have with it a sense of spatial and material relationship.

Well now, there is in fact nothing of this. I assert that if our life now consists of being in a room, this room is not —in its primary and proper reality—a space, nor is it anything material. This will produce in you such stupefaction that we can well leave the development of this extravagant idea for the next lecture.

Lesson V

Circumstances (surroundings) and what we know about them. Naked life and unthinking our thoughts. Circumstance (what lies about me) and I form a part of my life. The various things one does with circumstances. Thinking is not a primary 'doing'. Earlier presence of 'counting on'. The two ways of being of things; thinking them and living them. The primacy of interrogation and its pre-intellectual significance. Things are primarily conveniences and inconveniences. The emptiness of being.

I WAS ASSERTING that if our life now consists of being inside this room, the room is, in reality, not primarily and properly a space, or is it anything material.

Let us see if I can make this unusual idea into an evident truth for you.

You will remember how, and by what road, we arrived at this question. Having realized that our life now consists in the fact that I—the 'I' which is every one of you—am in this room, we wanted to clarify and to describe for ourselves the reality which lies behind the verb 'to be', the reality to which this verb alludes and which it designates. Evidently, this concerns the relationship between me and the room. We made various attempts to express that relationship in some way which, if not adequate, would at least be clear and satisfactory. First, we tried to understand it in a spatial sense: I form part of the room. But we saw quickly that this made no sense. I do not form part of this room because I—the I that lives in the life of every one of us—am unique. This room is completely heterogeneous to me, not by virtue of dissertations which would teach me that this room is a material space and I am not material (being made up also of soul and mind), but more basically because as I am unique, any other thing, whether matter or another spirit, is different from me, heterogeneous to me. In view of that, we get this negative result, that the phrase 'I being in this room' does not mean that I form part of it in any positive sense, and we said that it was the equivalent of 'I existing in something other than myself' or 'to exist outside myself'. But this, although true, was too abstract. 'To exist' is a highly abstract concept which we had to submit to semantic analysis. The result of this was that 'to exist', *sensu stricto*, means to achieve, to bring into being the essence, to be effectively what one is, *to be oneself.*

But this semantic result still leaves us too abstract, too remote, not sufficiently concrete in what we see clearly as constituting our present life, namely that I am in a room. And the other—to say that I exist outside myself—repels us in that 'outside' is a word denoting space which, in this case, becomes not only false, but absurd.

Lost in our search for clarity as to what 'being there' may mean, we perceive that we have been analyzing most of the terms in the phrase except the one that seemed to offer the smallest problem—the phrase 'this room'. We had left this unattended and intact because we thought that its meaning was perfectly clear, without any need for special analysis. But our error stemmed from this. We took as known that which the room represents as an ingredient in our life when the latter consists, as it does now, in being in the room. And we took it as known for the very reason that 'we know' many things about the room: that it is a space, that it is matter made up of atoms, and so on. All that we know *about* the room we ourselves put into it, and we now make it consist of this.

This, I said, is the general and stubborn error which hinders us and will continually hinder us in describing the great and terrible simplicity of our life, the failure to note the saving commonplace that everything we think about our life and its ingredients is something we do while in the midst of life; that this life, then, is there before we set ourselves to think *about* it and about those ingredients.

It is clear that in describing life now, we have set ourselves to think about it; but in this *single* case, what our thought will seek is to discover the vital reality in all its nakedness, to find what is when it is only that, when there is stripped from it all the other things we have been thinking about it which are not it. In short, in this *one* case, our thinking is forced to *unthink* all the other thoughts that we have been thinking about our life. (You will very shortly understand this phrase, which may now seem to you a paradox.

Of all our thoughts about our surroundings, the 'circumstancia', or world of our life, the most elemental and the one that thrusts itself at us with the greatest evidence is that the compass within which we find ourselves living is space. Therefore, on interpreting the expression 'our life now consists in our being in a room', we took it for granted that this room is undoubtedly a space. This inadvertent assumption is what has reacted on the rest of the phrase and has hindered us in getting its meaning straight.

The moment has come to emphasize something I said in the second lesson, when for the first time I gave a condensed description of what our life is, a description for which everything said later is only commentary and polishing.

I hope that at these heights none of you will confuse that reality which each of you calls 'his life' with his own being, his 'I'. I am no more than one ingredient in my life; the other is the surrounding circumstance, the world. My life, then, contains both of these within itself; but it is a reality distinct from me. *I live*, and, in living, I am in the surrounding circumstance, which is not I. The

reality of my being, my 'I', is, then, secondary to the integral reality which is my life; I find the former—the
reality of my 'I'—in the latter, the living reality. I and
circumstance both form parts of my life.

Now we can, without error, assert that I form a part
of something, namely of my life. The circumstance, the
surrounding—in this present case, the room—is the other
part of my life. It was a mistake to say that I—a part of
my life—form part of the other part of my life, which is
the room. No, I form part of the whole which is my life;
this is a whole for the very reason that I am a different
part from the other part which is the room. Thus, I said
in the second lesson, 'Our life is not only our person, but
also our world which forms a part of that life; it consists of the fact that the person is occupied by things
or with them, and evidently what our life is depends
as much on what our person is as on what our world
is. Neither the one nor the other is closer to us; we
do not first take account of ourselves and then of our surroundings, but living is, at root, a matter of finding ourselves confronting the world; with the world, within the
world, submerged in its trafficking, its problems, its web
of misfortunes. But the opposite is also true; that world,
being made up only of what affects each one of us, is inseparable from us. We are born with it, and world and
person are vitally like those pairs of divinities of ancient
Greece and Rome who were born together and lived together; the Dioscuri, the Heavenly Twins, for example,
Castor and Pollux, pairs of gods who were frequently
called *dii consentes*, the unanimous gods.'

Now, what we ask ourselves is 'What is this room?'.
But we ask it not merely in the abstract. We ask 'What is
this room?' in the sense that it is an ingredient in my life.
On finding himself alive, man finds himself *in* a circumstance, a set of surroundings, a world. In this case, the
circumstance consists of this room. My life now is my
being in a room. We ask ourselves what this thing is, in-

sofar as it is the thing in which I am.

Putting the question this way, in all strictness, we find that the answer is extremely simple and formidably commonplace; it is, at the same time, also fundamental, and it will suddenly illumine very decisive things for us.

Note well, that for me to be in this room is not the same as for me to be thinking in or about this room.

To think in or about something is not only something I do, but it is one of the many things that I can do with something. I can, for instance, come into this room or go out of it—these are two things I can do with it. Also, I can, once I have entered it, stay in it a minute or an hour; this staying is another thing I can do with it. One must distrust the relative aspect, and even the absolutely passive aspect, which words sometimes present. One could say that staying is not doing in that all doing implies activity. Nevertheless, as I can at any moment leave the room, my staying in it implies that I do this for some positive, active reason, so that simply staying in it is as much 'doing' as is coming out or going in—as much, indeed, as such energetic acts as building it or destroying it. Each new moment that you stay in this hall is *doing* that—staying, remaining, in the fullest meaning of that activity. And when, a short time ago, you stood at the door of this hall waiting to enter, you were also doing something—'killing time before entering the hall'; the phrase, as you now see, is not metaphorical but direct and exact. To kill time is an effective, energetic doing, neither more nor less so than making a bargain, making a meal, making a table, making verses, making illusions for oneself. And it is evident that your waiting at the door was a kind of doing in that you could have not waited but could have come in or burst into the hall ahead of time; or, in order to save time, you could have taken pains to reach the door at the exact moment when the lesson was to begin in order not to lose time. He who came early did so because he had time, and because he had it, he could set himself to 'kill it', that is, to wait, just as he who has money can make a bargain with it, or make a house, and just as he who has poetry (that is, the poetic talent) can make verses.

So the things we can do in this room, with this room, are innumerable; or, to put it better, our possible activities, our *doings* with it, with respect to it, in it, or about it, are beyond number. One of these, one of many, consists in setting ourselves to think in it or about it.

Well then, the strange thing about this kind of doing that we call 'thinking about something' arises from the fact that it can never be our primary, primitive action with that something. What I am saying is that the first thing we do about something can never be thinking about it; in order for me to be able to engage in this peculiar activity, the thing I deal with must have been involved in a previous relationship with me which was not merely a matter of thinking about it. Thus, in order for me to think about this room, I must previously have entered it, or at least have heard talk about it. For one of the things we can do with something is 'to hear talk about it'; the proof of this is that when something is antipathetic or offensive to us we usually say, 'We don't even want to hear about it'. This implies that in other cases, our hearing is a desiring to hear, that is, a lending of attention, a process of making ourselves attentive.

But it will be said that those things that I do with the room before I think about it also imply, in their turn, thinking. To enter the room, to stay in it, to remain standing or seated in it, or to walk about it—these assume in themselves an awareness of the room or, as has been said for three centuries, a 'being conscious of it'. Is not this recognition a matter of thinking? This question is going to occupy us in depth; it is the great ideological battle in which we will be engaging. But now, as for this description of our lives which we are making as a preamble to metaphysics, it is enough for us to remember that distinction between *contar con* (count on) and *reparar* (to observe, to be conscious of). You will remember that whichever it is, even to think the least bit about something is to be conscious of it. Or, what is the same thing, thought is, at the very least, a 'being conscious of'. I do not pay attention to the armchair in which I am sitting, we said; but I count on it, I rely on it. If any one moves it, I am aware that something about it has changed, that previously it was different; and, nevertheless, previously, I paid no attention to it. It existed for me then, but not consciously. It was there in front of me. It constituted a present element of my life in that earlier 'now', I had been aware of it. In short, I was conscious of it but I did not think about it.

So it is false to say that everything I do with something implies a genuine thinking about that something or a being conscious of it. If we men, who must fasten or unfasten our numerous buttons several times a day, had to think about or be conscious of each one of those buttons and each of the buttonholes every time we did it, we would need almost a full working day for the operation, and, at the end, we would be far more exhausted than if we had been taking part in a series of lessons in metaphysics.

To sum up, thinking about something is an act of ours that always assumes other activities of ours with that something; these latter are not thinking, but imply only that simple 'taking account of', that strange presence within my consciousness of everything that forms part of my life. But this primary presence of everything I depend on in living is not the same as the very special form in which an object of consciousness appears before the subject that is conscious of it, in which what is thought is there in the presence of the one who thinks about it.

Well now, the root and seed of the entire modern age has been a belief which is directly contrary to what I have been saying. The modern age was formed around the basic assertion that our primary relationship with things is thinking about them and, therefore, that things are originally what they are when we think them. That is what has been called 'idealism', and the whole modern period—in its philosophy and in everything else—has, in essence, been idealism.

This suggests to you the importance that may lie in this simple statement which we have just made—that things are primordially what they are when we are *not* thinking of them, before we are thinking of them; they are what they are when we are counting on them, taking them for granted, when we simply live them.

Putting the matter thus, one notes that we cannot understand these two modes of the being of things—the primary, or what they are when we are not thinking of them, and the secondary, or what they are when we do think of them—unless we confront and compare the one with the other.

Well now, what is a thing first, when we first think of it, in the very first moment of any thought about it? For example, take this light. Imagine that we set ourselves to think about this light, and that we carry our thought to the utmost that man can achieve today in this order of thinking; that is, that we have thought about that light everything that man today can think about it. That maximum limit of thought about light is called optics. We will, then, have created optics. And if we observe the end result of such a vast and complex operation of thinking, of such a sharp and precise activity, we will note that what we find at the end of optics is sufficient knowledge of what light is.

At the end of optics, then, we do not have this light, but we have a very different thing which is 'the being of light'. When we have this, we say that we know. To know is to possess the being of a thing; not the thing itself, but its being. As this possesion is verified in a thought which thinks that being, we say that our thought is true.

Later, we must talk a great deal about all this; but for the moment, we will rest content with what has been said because this allows us to answer the question we were asking a moment ago—'What is a thing first, when we first set ourselves to think about it? not what is it before thinking of it, but when one starts to think about it?' If the end and the fulfillment of my thinking about it is to know *what it is*, obviously, my thinking about it will begin by not knowing what it is. Thinking, which culminates in knowing, begins by not knowing. Thought, then, before knowing, is pure ignorance. Yet he who does not think is not ignorant—the stone is not ignorant about the dynamite that breaks it—because being ignorant is thinking positively about something, is thinking that one does not possess the being of a thing, is thinking that one does not know what it is, in short, is thinking that one does not know. Ignorance knows that a thing has a being but does not know what that being is, does not know what the thing is. But 'what is' has an originating and interrogative meaning of its own. What is this light? Here is our first thought about the light, our initial ignorance. It is a question. And for that first thought, this *thing* is . . . a questionable thing, a problem. The first thing that a thing is when we think about it is . . . a question.

By the time we reached this fifth lesson, we had already made certain experiments with the style of this course which we must use to good account, enriching you as well as me. In the beginning, when you heard certain expressions of mine, you thought more than once, 'Well, this is said metaphorically or, at least, not in a strict and formal sense'. Then you began to correct this; those same phrases that seemed metaphorical and informal began to have a direct and precise meaning. This is what happens to us now in this case.

I say that when we think about them, things are first of

all . . . questions. Before I knew the least detail about this light, before I could say that this light is this, that, or the other thing, I had to make a question out of it, had to ask myself, 'What is it?' Everything else that it might be would come later, after its questioned being, after its being as a question. *Because* something is a question to me, my thought begins working in order to solve the question. If not, my thought would not function, would not have any reason to set itself in motion, and though I might have it as a mechanism at my disposal, as a 'faculty', I would not make use of it.

First, then, things are questions for my thinking, something with regard to which one asks questions. Well, but that question 'What is light?'—to whom is it addressed? To ask is an act of mine. It is I who question. Good, but every question about something is addressed to someone. To whom do I address this particular question? To myself? Or to someone else; for example, to a physicist?

Let us make this first case clearer. In this, I ask the question of *myself*. But is this not strange? Apparently it is a matter of one part of me asking a question of another part of me, as if we were to say—and this *is* a metaphor—that one lobe of my brain asks another lobe of my brain, 'Look, friend, what do you think about this?'.

There is, in fact, a bit of this. I direct my question to the only part of me that can answer, the only part that has a voice, that can speak—I direct it to my intellect. Every question, as such, is an intellectual question. But this assumes that the interrogatory I, the I that questions its intellect, is not the intellectual, and if this nonintellectual 'I' propounds the question to the intellect, this means that things are already questions for it, but in a preintellectual sense.

Let us not lose ourselves in this tangle which is, perhaps, the first real one we meet in this course, the first which is difficult to understand. Let us take a fresh look at the terms of the matter.

For something to be a question means that we seek (*questio* comes from *querere*, to seek) to know what it is, we seek its being. But if we seek the being of a thing, this means that we were previously involved in a relationship with the thing, that we had it. I have this light here, now, and, hence, it occurs to me to ask myself what it is, what its being is. It would never occur to me to ask myself about the being of a thing that I did not have here. Precisely. But now, let us look at the opposite side of the matter. When I have the thing, 'this light', I do not have its being; for that, I must search. Then, the thing I have, the things that are here and that make up my surroundings, are different from this being.

But—and here comes the tremendous paradox—if this light, here, is something other than its being, this means that things have no 'being' until I ask about it and make my thought function. But just as thinking of these—as we know—is only one of the innumerable things I can do with them, the result will be that in all the rest of my actions, all the rest of my vital relations with things, these have no being. And now we begin to ask ourselves loudly 'What the devil!' and then to say, 'When I am not thinking about things, but am living with them without thinking about them, what are they? What are things when they have no being, that is, when they are . . . not?'

I am sure you have given yourselves the answer and with all the necessary evidence; but, at that point, you have refused to accept it because you thought it absurd and unintelligible. To my question, 'What are things when we are not thinking of them, when for that reason they have no being, in short, when they are *not?*', you will have answered 'Ah, then, things are . . . nothing'.

But, of course, this seems senseless to you, and you go on, 'So this light which is lighted for me is . . . nothing when I am not thinking about it? But did we not, in the same argument, say that it is here, that it gives us light, and so on? How can we add that it is nothing?' That first statement in this lesson—that if our life now consists in being in this room, this room is not primarily a material space—was stupefying enough. But this present one— 'when I am not thinking about it, this light which shines on me is nothing'—sets one's hair on end.

I am well aware that the matter becomes difficult to understand. Therefore, I need you to help me. And to do this, I need you to decide to fulfill your unspoken promise by putting aside everything you were thinking *about* the light and holding exclusively to what the light is. And so, what is it? Well, now that it is shining on me, it is what I can light and put out, what costs the faculty a certain amount of money, and so on. Good; but none of this is the being of this light. When I think about it a great deal and finally come to the end of my optical investigation, I discover that the being of the light consists of vibrations of the ether. What has this—vibrations of the ether—to do with its shining on me now, with the fact that I can light it and put it out, with the other fact that it costs the faculty money? All this says more about me than about the light. Strictly speaking, it describes only what happens to me with regard to the light—being lighted by it—and what happens to it with regard to me —that it shines on me. But it says nothing more about the light itself, not even the least thing about what this light is. Its ether vibration is not here; it does not happen to me, nor does it happen to the light through me. Therefore, while my action in regard to it, what happens to me from it, is a matter of receiving its light so that I can read, lighting it for this purpose or putting it out so it shall not cost the faculty too much, and so on, this light is neither vibrations of the ether nor any of these other things.

Let us now go on to answer our question directly and precisely—that question, 'What is this light when I am not thinking about it?'. It is what shines on me and lets me read, what I light and then put out, what costs the faculty a certain sum. But—nothing more? Nothing more; that is to say, that much and no more. Or, to put it another way, to be all that is to be nothing.

I do not pretend that you will, for the time being, completely understand what I have just said. In this course, it has happened more than once that when I took a new step in describing life, you did not, at the moment, understand it very well. Nevertheless, the new idea, even when it first appeared, produced in you a glimmering of the fact that a certain unsuspected truth lay ahead for which it would be useful to prepare a bright light. This preparation, this 'Watch out!' is enough for the moment. The light is foretold by the glimmer.

What is important for us to keep fully clear is that if our life consists of what we do, we can divide that into two parts: on the one hand, all we do with things aside from thinking about them and on the other, quite separate, that most peculiar form of doing which is thinking. You will note that the division separates our lives into two very unequal sectors in that, on the one side, there is only that form of doing which is thinking and, on the other, there are all the other innumerable forms of doing which make up our existence. Thinking is neither more nor less a form of doing than any of the others; yet if we believe it useful to set it at one side, this is because, as we will see, only when we engage in it do things take on a being which they do not have in their other relationships with us.

Now you need to become accustomed to the effort of thinking how things are when and while you are not thinking about them and to exercise yourselves in that effort.

Imagine that a short time ago, in place of choosing this light as an example, we had chosen the earth and had said to ourselves, 'What is this earth that I see with my eyes, that I tread with my feet, on which I walk slowly at times and quickly at other times?'. While we were thinking all this, we were occupied with the earth and not the light. But though we were paying no attention to it, the light was shining on us, and, thanks to its brilliance, we could read. I was not paying attention to it, but I was depending on it, on its lighting me, just as I am not observing this chair, but I do count on the kind service it renders me by giving me a place to sit. If we now want to express the reality of what the light is and what this chair is, we will have to say, 'The reality of this light at this moment consists entirely in shining on me, and the reality of the chair consists of its being what I am sitting on. Outside of this present and actual shining on me, this action in relation to me, this light is, at the moment, nothing in my life.' And, as we are talking only of what our life is and what its ingredients may be, I have the right to say that things are primarily only their pure and present action in regard to me. The light shines, it illumines me, and this is all.

But suddenly the light goes out, and I, who was at that moment occupied with the earth and not the light, stop what I am doing when its lighting ceases and set to work with the light. I need to go on reading, and the light denies me its habitual service. My life, which consisted then of reading, is disturbed and set at naught by the lack of light; it is converted into something else, into another situation, another life made up of not being able to read —because there is no light—a life made up of a negation. This negation of my life which I find in my life, this not being able to be what I need to be, namely, a reader, makes me recognize that I am not coinciding with my environment (my circumstance), that this is different from me, that I cannot 'count on it' that it is strange and alien to me. In short, that I am estranged.

It is when our environment fails us in something that we feel it to be strange, like something other than ourselves, and it is then, when it fails us, when it is suddenly strange to us—precisely then—that we notice it. It is when this light goes out that we turn our attention to it

and ask ourselves, 'What is happening to this light?', a
question that carries within itself the other 'What is this
light?'. When the light does not shine and I need it to
shine, when it does not do for me what it was doing and
what made me comfortable, then the light does something new to me; it makes me uncomfortable and, in
making me uncomfortable, it makes itself . . . a question for me.

If everything that surrounds me, beginning with my
body, were comfortable for me, I would not be aware of
anything, I would not feel my surroundings as surroundings, as something strange to me, but I would believe that
the world was I, myself. If, when I moved my hand toward the table, this latter gave way and offered no resistance, no negative response to the movement of my hand,
I would have a right to feel and to think that my hand
and the table both belonged to me, that they were I. But
if the table did behave that way when I, for my part,
needed to rest my arms on it, its giving way would
annoy me, and I would feel it to be strange. When a
thing annoys me, it poses a question to me; because I
need it and cannot 'count on it', because it fails me. It is
when things are lacking that they begin to have a being.
Apparently, it is the being of things that is lacking in our
lives, that creates the enormous emptiness in life which
thought, in its incessant effort, works eagerly to fill.

Lesson VI

Revision of the itinerary. The repertory of possibilities in the environment. Destiny and liberty. To live is to exist here and now.

LET US FIRST gather together briefly all the discoveries we have made so that we can resume our itinerary.

If we were occupying ourselves with astronomy, our project would be to define the being of the stars, to find out what the stars are. Similarly, the intent of these lessons is to try to define the being of man. Man's being is what is customarily called his life. We are our lives. Now, the life of every one of us consists, for the moment, in finding himself having to exist in a circumstance, an environment, a world, or whatever else you choose to call it. That circumstance, that world, in which, like it or not, we have to live, we cannot choose; but without our leave and without knowing how it happened, we find ourselves tossed into it, shipwrecked in it, and, in order to sustain ourselves, we have no choice but to keep doing something, to come forth, swimming.

I do not give myself life, but it is given to me; I find myself with it on finding myself with myself. But what is given to me when I am given life is the inexorable necessity of having to do something under the threat of ceasing to live. And not even in this am I free—because ceasing to live is also a form of doing; it is killing myself regardless of the weapon, whether it be a rifle, or hunger and exhaustion. The life that was given to me was not given to me ready-made; I must make it for myself. It was not given to me in finished form, as existence is given

89

to the star or the stone, all fixed and without problems. What is given to me with life, then, is nothing but the need to do things. *Life gives one a great deal to do.*

And the most serious thing about these tasks that make up life is not that one has to do them, but that before doing anything I, myself, must decide what I am going to do; therefore, what I am going to be. When we reached this point, I asked you to note the superlative paradox that it involves because, according to this, man's being, unlike that of all the other things in the universe, consists not in what he already is but in what he is going to be; therefore, in what he not yet is. Man begins by being his future, his time to come. Thus, life is an operation which is performed toward that which lies ahead.

How can this be made to agree with my statement that life is always a present, a now?

Let me say once more that life consists in what we do, in our occupations. Always, we must be occupied with something, and we have already seen that this includes doing nothing—waiting, killing time—which is an occupation and, at times, an anguishing one. But these occupations, to which we dedicate our lives, do not come as imposed upon us. We have to solve now the question of what we will be busy about then, in a moment. That is to say, we are now busy deciding our future occupation. When this is a matter of our daily existence, formed by habits that are well-grooved, this decision is easy. He who goes daily to talk with friends at a certain hour does not ordinarily hesitate very much in deciding to do that because that also is an occupation—let us not argue whether good or bad—it is passing the time, which is the opposite of killing time. He who waits, we said, is making time *for* something, but he who simply lets time pass is losing time—unmaking it.

I insist then, that now—in every now—we are occupied in deciding on our future occupation, that which we are not yet, that which we are going to be. Well now, that is occupying oneself by anticipation; it is being pre-occupied. Life is preoccupation, and it is always this, at every moment, and not only in particularly serious oc-cupations, though then the character of the preoccupa-tion closest to our lives unhappily shows itself most clearly; this is inevitable in a being like man who must decide his own being and what he is going to be.

Well now, what we call preoccupation, this busying ourselves in advance with what we are going to be doing, is nothing but occupying ourselves with the future. And man is that strange being who has the privilege—at once painful and wonderful—of occupying himself with the future. Now, at this moment, where are we, you and I? Strictly speaking, you, at this present moment, are *not* amid the present, but you are waiting for the next word that I am going to pronounce; you are in the immediate future, leaning toward it, attentive to it. What I have just said, the present which you have already heard, no longer occupies you. As for me, I am now preoccupied with the sentence I am going to pronounce; what I am now saying no longer occupies me, my larynx and my lips pronounce it almost mechanically. At this moment, I cannot let my-self sketch the substantial philosophic problems which this important subject demands. Let us rest content only with this; that life is, now and forever, its own prow, making its own bow wave, anticipating the foaming fu-ture and cutting into it, deciding what it is going to be.

But if I must decide, willing or not, what I am going to do—in that nobody can hand me that decision—this means that life always, *always* sets me face to face with various possibilities of doing this or that. When I leave here, I *can* do many different and varied things. Among them I must make my decision. Having to decide implies that my being is never decided ahead of time, as is the being of the star to which is given its orbit that is already fixed. Before coming to a decision, I am, then, undecided, perplexed. Hence, life is . . . perplexity, constant and essential perplexity.

THIS IS THE PLACE we have come to, and, therefore, this is where we must dig in our toes in order to begin moving forward again.

And let us start by asking ourselves, 'What is it that must happen?', 'How must things be so that one feels himself perplexed?', or, to put it another way, 'What are the ingredients of that perplexity which is the true substance of our lives?'. It is apparent that in order to feel perplexed, one must have to be doing something, but when he finds himself facing so many different possibilities of doing, or being, he does not know which to choose. Thus, the symbol of perplexity is the crossroads; with several paths open before us, which shall we take? One of them leads us to being one thing, another to being another thing; we are to choose nothing less than our very being. And, I repeat, this, with a greater or lesser degree of drama, is happening at every moment of our lives. Man's existence is a constant crossroads.

The circumstance, the environment, the world into which we have fallen on coming to life and in which we are prisoners and perplexed, is in every case composed of a certain repertory of possibilities, of being able to do this, that, or the other. Faced with this keyboard of possible things to do, we are free to prefer one or another; but the keyboard, as a whole, is fateful. Surrounding circumstances make up the circle of fatality which forms part of that reality which we call life. And, because this is the basic characteristic of our existence, note and remember that this fateful character of our surroundings, of the world in which we live, does not oblige us to do or to be any one single thing. Would that it did! Then man's life would be like the life of the stone, very comfortable, because existence for the stone is directed by cosmic forces. The stone we throw into the air feels no perplexity whatsoever; what it is going to do, what it is going to be, has been forever decided—it will fall toward the center of the earth. But in what direction you are going to walk has not been decided, nor is it even decided whether tomorrow you will meditate a bit on what I have been saying to you or will misunderstand it. You can do the one or the other. Within the destiny marked out by your environment, you are free; even more, you are fatefully free because you have no choice, like it or not, but to select your future within the range and margin that your fateful environment offers you.

Every man—and, of course, every woman—has his or her world, the environment which seems more or less like that of his neighbors but which always contains certain different elements. Most of you who are here are Spaniards, and being a Spaniard means having an environment, a destiny, and a repertory of possibilities which are different from those of an Englishman or a German. But even though we are Spaniards, our surroundings would be very different if we were living in the Spain of the seventeenth century. The world in which we exist perforce is not only a specific 'here', but it also has a definite date. To live is to exist here and now; as I said before, to emerge swimming in the here and now rather than in any imaginary environment. Hence, everyone who does not begin by accepting this world gladly, in all its effective reality, should seem to us idiotic. Face to face with destiny, the only sensible thing that can be done is to accept it. That comes first, and then we would see if we can in any way improve this environment so as to get the best possible out of it. Life is always a place and a date—it is the contrary of utopianism and timelessness—or, what is the same thing, life in itself is historical.

I think that on reaching this point you can see with a certain clarity and a greater precision that statement in which we were defining the problem of life—the life of each one of you—by saying that it consists in the fact that the 'I' which is each of us must exist in a circumstance, in a given set of surroundings within which we must realize ourselves. Note it well—it consists in the fact that I must be I, not within myself, but in the world where, willy-nilly, I find myself, in the world of now, and that my world will be able to offer me, more or less, facilities for realizing myself within it, but that it will always be different and separate from me.

Lesson VII

The general structure of our life and its components. What kind of 'doing' is thinking about something? To think, to say, a commonplace. The necessity of being.

WITH ALL THIS, we have done no more than define the general structure of our life. But if what I have said is true, at each specific moment of our life we will have a particular case of that general structure; that is, if at any moment we analyze our own reality, we will find it made up of these stated components—it will consist of our being in a definite environment, of our doing something in this environment, occupying ourselves with something. This 'doing', this occupation of ours, was decided upon by us in a preoccupation, and if we decided to do what we are doing, it was because this seemed to fulfill the 'I' that each one of us here knows that he must be. Man cannot, materially, take a single step without anticipating his entire future and, in view of this deciding, to take that step or not, to move in this direction or that.

All this is actually happening right now; your life now consists precisely in being in this room, and it was the attempt to analyze this very concrete situation, to work out its anatomy almost microscopically in order to find full evidence of all those substantive ingredients of life, which made us catch a glimpse of those macroscopic statements.

Our project, then, is to express in concepts, to think out the reality which is our life such and as it now is. But we met a fundamental difficulty; this is that on thinking of his life man tends—for reasons which we will in good

95

time discover—to think of it not as it is, but to interpret it as if the being of that life were of the same structure as is the being of the corporeal things that we find in our lives [1].

ON REACHING this point, I would like to summarize the other things I said in Lesson V, and go ahead as quickly as possible.

And to this end, I would like you to ask yourselves, 'What kind of "doing" is it to think about a thing? That is, what are we doing with the thing when we think about it?' You will not hesitate in answering: 'When we think about a thing, what we are doing is to occupy ourselves with finding out what it is, with discovering its being'. Of course; but this implies that the thing— whatever and however it is in my life, does not show its being before I think about it, or, what is the same thing, it is in my life, it acts in it, but it has no being. This light shines on me, I possess its illumination, so I have it as a light but I do not have its being; its being is not there, I do not know *what it is*. And this occurs to me with everything else that makes up my life.

What happens—and we will see why—is that we have already thought about many things, and we have received still more thoughts about them which have been accumulated by the educative tradition and the surrounding culture. Therefore, we might believe that we know more than a little about them, about what they are, and this knowing has become such a habit that their being— which we already know—seems to us to be right here. Thus, when we say that this room *is* a material space, it seems to us that this—a material space—is here by itself and without our thinking about it. And, nevertheless, it is clear enough that, strictly speaking, neither you nor I

1. At this point in the manuscript, a note in the margin says 'Re-reading of the first pages of Lesson V' [*Compilers' note*].

nor anyone else knows truly and absolutely what a material space *is*. We know about it only something that is very partial, approximate, and problematical. And if, even after humanity has thought about it for thousands and thousands of years, nobody has succeeded in knowing fundamentally *what it is,* how can it be here, forming part of my life? You remember that everything that forms a part of my life is manifest, patent; if not, I am not living it.

If the surroundings or circumstance in which we are submerged—and this submergence is what we call life—should have a being, and to live would then be to find that being clear before us, man's existence would be the very opposite of what it is. In the first place, we would not have to think about things, but they would reveal their being to us by themselves and in their appearance before us; that is, living would then be knowing what the world is, and, in knowing this, we would know its past and its future; and, in knowing the world's future, we would know our own future in it rather than finding ourselves amid perplexity, having to decide among various possibilities what that future of ours is. A world whose being is known is composed solely of necessities.

But the fact is that the basic reality which we call life has characteristics that are totally contrary to these. Always, when we say of something that 'it *is* thus' or '*is* so', '*is* this' or '*is* that other way', we have abandoned the thing as it first appeared before us and have substituted a thought of our own, an interpretation. The thing in itself, on its first arrival in our lives, is neither thus nor so, this way nor that; it is, in short, naked of any being. The earth is here beneath my feet or under the foundations of the building in which I find myself. It has, in my life, a primary role which is to uphold and sustain me. But suddenly it shakes, moves from side to side, ceases to be firm and to sustain me. It is then that I make a question of it. Before then, it was—note this—that which sustained me. Now it is . . . a question, a problem. I ask myself, 'What *is* the earth?'. Thought begins to function, spurred on by the vital, pre-intellectual urgency of having to be upheld by the earth and having it fail me, having this life-long need of mine betrayed. If the world about me were responding to all my needs, I would never have raised a question about any part of it; it would never have occurred to me to think about it; nor would I even have had the idea of needing it. A world so favorable in that sense is another world, a world of which man dreams, and he dreams of it for the very reason that the existing world is just the opposite—a world unfavorable to man.

In man's secret depths, he is always aware of that resistance of the world to him, but he is very slow to reveal his own secret to himself. It may seem strange that one can have a secret from oneself, yet there is nothing simpler, or more common. Everything we rely on is a secret, everything that intervenes in our life, but we have told no one about it, or, what is the same thing, we have not thought about it. As we will see, to think and to say are the same thing, and it is no mere chance that in Greek, *logos* should mean both things. The thought does not exist without the word; it is essential that thought be expressly formulated. That which is unexpressed, unformulated, that which is mute, has not been thought, and, as it has not been thought, it is not known, and it remains secret. Therefore, to speak—that is, to think—is to make manifest, to declare or to clarify, to discover, what is covered or hidden, to reveal the arcane. 'To say', to say something is to make manifest that which previously existed in a latent and larval form. And the primary meaning of saying is not conversing, it is not my revealing my thought to another, a thought which, when not revealed by language, is for the other a secret, something hidden; in order for me to be able to say something to someone, I must previously have said it to myself; that is, I have thought it, and there is no thinking unless I am talk-

ing to myself. The result is that before revealing something to my neighbor, I must have revealed it to myself.

But for this, it is necessary for me, in addition to noting it, to have paid attention to it, to have made a question of it, to have defined it. Language is in itself a science, the primogenial science which I find already made
in my social environment; it is the elemental knowledge
which I receive from the community in which I live and
which then imposes on me an interpretation of things, a
repertory of opinions about their being. Language is, par
excellence, the commonplace, the vagrant, casual knowledge in which all my own thought, original and genuine,
must inexorably have its dwelling.

But let us go back to the matter in hand. I said that in
his own hidden depths, man always takes account of the
antagonistic character which the world has toward him,
but that he is very slow in revealing this secret to himself; in short, slow in thinking it and saying it, in knowing it directly and expressly. But man customarily has
two ways of expressing and of thinking about what
makes up his life, that is, those things on which he
counts. One way is direct, the other indirect. For example, when man invents the myth of the magic wand and
with it a magic world wherein all his desires come true
without effort or resistance, he is not defining directly
the real world in which he lives as a world in which those
desires are not realized or which at least imposes grievous
efforts for the satisfaction of our desires. But in the act of
imagining that myth, he expresses to himself indirectly
this fact in secret and without knowing it; he is aware of
an unfavorable and antimagic world, that is, a world
composed of ingredients that fail him, that do not serve
him. The magic world is an imaginary circumstance in
which everything would serve us, in which the earth
would never tremble. In this world, man would feel an
unshakable sense of security. But if he imagines it, this is

because in the real world, the world that man has no need to imagine but which inexorably involves and imprisons him, he feels himself insecure, a stranger, and lost. The tale of the magic wand expresses, then, in positive form and as though in relief, the unexpressed, secret presence, and, to put it this way, the great emptiness which the resistance of the world has in his life.

Before the earth failed us with its shaking, we had not thought about it; we simply used it as we use this room by being in it [2].

Earlier, we were resting on the earth, sustaining ourselves on it; but when it becomes that which fails to uphold us, we do not know *what to do* with the earth, what to look for in regard to it. And we do not know the latter because we do not know the former. So that becomes a question for us. Fundamentally, the question is one of our behavior toward it, our conduct, what we do with the earth. But for this, we need to be quite sure that we are paying proper heed to it; and for this, it is necessary that the earth have a conduct, a being. Toward the earth, we are disoriented for the very reason that it has no being and, therefore, one must search for it. For its own sake, the earth does not need to have a being; it is we who need that it have such a thing. Does this mean that the being *of* things becomes one of man's necessities?

Out of this arises the question, 'What *is* the earth?' [3].

2. That which refuses us its service, says 'No' to us, is opposed to us. The world is born to us as a 'No'. One retires to the Aventine, the strike, a discovery of the working world. The magic world would not be a world without me, myself: God. It is not that His thinking would be to create; God does not think [*Author's note, in the margin*].

3. As the reader will observe, the two preceding lessons and others that follow are shorter than the others; and the editing of the manuscript becomes more synthetic and implicit. Remember that these pages reproduce a text prepared for university lessons on metaphysics and that in every case, the oral exposition might differ from the prepared manuscript [*Compilers' note*].

Lesson VIII

The question of being. The myth of the expulsion from Paradise. Method and the contemplative life. The theories of 'doing' confront the emptiness of being. Resort to the social 'I' of the people. The assumptions of this resort. From nothing to nobody. The system of essential actions. Antagonism between tradition and reason. Again, what is the earth? Again, the immateriality of circumstance, environment; its usefulness.

IF THE EARTH SHAKES, ceasing to uphold us, thereby denying us its habitual service, we ask ourselves, 'What *is* the earth? '. When the sun suddenly, and in full daylight, refuses its habitual illumination so favorable to men, the latter ask, 'What *is* the sun? '.

This question about being comes, then, inspired by having lost confidence in our surroundings; this is what we do when we do not know what to do about something, how to behave, what line of conduct to follow. Our previous confidence consisted in our not having paid attention to the thing as such, in our not having seen it as another thing, independent, foreign, and strange to us. When it fails us, we see this failure as a resistance to us, as a denial of ourselves, and this being which is not 'I' separates it from me, sets it up in opposition to me; and this characteristic of being 'what is against me' makes me see it as independent of me, puts it within itself.

The same thing happens with my body. When it is sick, it is opposed to me and does not serve me. *Ipso facto*, it remains foreign to me, different from me. Thus, man, as he lives, discovers the basic duality of his life; he feels that he is amid something other than himself, in a foreign country, *dépaysé*.

Perhaps the myth of the expulsion from Paradise represents this characteristic of life which puts it outside an environment that would not resist us and thereby would be confused with our very selves; in other words, it would not be an environment. The world into which man is thrown when he comes out of Paradise is the real world, for it is composed of resistences to man, of things surrounding him that he does not know what to do with because he does not know what aspect of them to study. Paradise is the magic world of which we were talking the other day. The real world, on the contrary, is the anti-Paradise. Confidence in the habitual, in the things one pays no attention to, is replaced by lack of confidence, disorientation, an incessant watchfulness.

Such circumstances, such surroundings, composed of things toward which we do not know how to act, are made up of problems, of questions. What is primarily a question for us is what we will do when faced by an earth that trembles, an earth which is *not* quiet, a sun that does *not* shine, a body that, being ill, is not well. Therefore, the first question for us is what we should do, our own actions. And note the result, which is almost funny; on facing the question of what we will do with those things, what we decide is to make a question about them, asking ourselves, 'What is this earth? What is this sun? What is my body?'.

But let us go a bit further into the meaning of this making a question of things. Does it not also include making for ourselves a question about our action? When the earth trembles, I do not know whether to break into a run or to stand still, to climb a tree or to rush to the sea in flight from the rebellious earth. And in order to solve this question of my material activities in regard to it, I ask myself the question about the being of the earth; that is, I make for myself a question of what I *ought to think* about it—hence, a question concerning another act of mine; but now it is the strange intellectual act. So I suspend my corporeal, let us say my practical, treatment of the earth, and I busy myself with an intellectual treatment of it. When the rest of my life becomes a question, I shut myself up in another dimension of my life—thought. This other dimension has been called 'the contemplative life'.

The name leads to an error. Thought, as one of man's activities, does not consist in looking disinterestedly at the objects about one and reflecting them as does a mirror, which is what the word 'contemplation' means.

We have seen that the initial act of thought was to ask about the being of something, for example, of the earth that trembled. But the earth is here, and so I do not have to ask myself about it. On the contrary, the question means that I need to separate myself from the earth, which is here, and set myself in motion toward its being, which is not here. Hence, we have one of the most insistent metaphors which describes thought as a process of traveling and pictures the man who thinks as a traveler, a *viator*. This idea of a road to be traveled culminates in the idea of *method*. So thought is not a contemplation of the earth which is already here but, on the contrary, an attempt to cease seeing the earth as it is and to substitute another thing which is its being. The other and more modern metaphor used to describe the intellectual act, thought, is this—out of the earth which is here and which is trembling, which fails to serve us and prevents us from being certain of it, we must make another earth which is more sure. If, with respect to these earthquakes, I know what to watch out for, if I know when, why, and in what degree they are produced, I acquire a certain sense of security about them. But that assumes that I use the earth which is here as a datum or a group of data with which, as with matter, I can contrast a firm image of the earth, the being of the earth, the truth about the earth.

Seen through this metaphor, thought is not contemplation; it is construction, and it appears like a particular case of technical work, which is not disinterested, not a matter of reflecting things, but of transforming them by making with them another thing that may serve me and is adapted to my needs. As the carpenter takes the log of wood which the tree offers to him (and which is here) and makes out of it a chair which is not 'here' but which is a creation, a construction of his, so thought takes the immediate things of our life and makes their being, which soothes us and allows us to use them, we might say against their will.

Without insisting further on this theme, it is well to emphasize that this incidental example gives us a glimpse of all thought, including that which pretends to be purely contemplative, as a particular case of man's technical activity. If this were certain, it would have, in some way, to invert the traditional order, saying that man does not fabricate tools and instruments because he thinks and knows, but that, on the contrary, he is *Homo sapiens* because he is, like it or not, *Homo faber*, and truth, theory, knowing are nothing but technical products. And in fact of the many things that are made out of the wood of the tree—chairs, tables, statues, crosses, canoes—one is the theory that can be made, be fabricated, about the wood of a tree. More than that, one cannot make even the simplest small table out of it unless one has previously made a small theory about it. The smallest table does assume certain elemental ideas of aesthetics.

So my question, 'What is the earth?', expresses my lack of sureness with respect to that most important ingredient of my surroundings. Earlier, being then full of confidence, I counted on the earth without paying any attention to it; now, when it shakes, I think about it, but I cannot depend on it for the simple reason that I no longer *have* the earth. I used to call 'earth' that which upheld me; but now it no longer upholds me, and, therefore, it is not earth. (*Terra, tersa,* is the 'dry thing', that which is not liquid, but solid and firm.) What is left for us? I cannot remain content with the one or the other; the earth is neither the one nor the other. When, for the first time, I find the earth as something apart from myself, no longer docile in my service, the first thing I find is that it has *no* being; or, what is the same thing, that to me it is a nonbeing. Therefore, I say that I do not *have* the earth, but that in its place I have something devoid of being. And how am I going to know what I can do with the earth if it consists in not being this or that, if it is, therefore, pure enigma? The earth undoubtedly goes on being there; there is such a thing, but it is a nonbeing.

Perhaps this becomes a bit difficult for you to understand, but it is the simplest thing in the world. Imagine that to someone who does not know the Chinese language we hand a paper written in that tongue and say to him, 'If you do not do what it says in that paper you will die tomorrow'. The written thing is there in front of him; there it is, a message. But what does the message say? It says . . . nothing intelligible. What is before him, then, is a negation, a void, the absence of a message. There is undoubtedly a reality, but this positive reality consists precisely in a negation of itself; this is what philosophy used to call 'privation', an active nonbeing.

Our question, 'What is the earth?', tries to fill this void, to find beyond this 'nonbeing' of the earth its positive being, to replace with a sense of security the feeling of unsureness which we experienced.

Let us now see what our second act is after that first act which consisted in questioning ourselves.

The anguish that man feels in the midst of an earthquake cannot be minimized: every man feels it on his own, most individual account. The wish to emerge from this unease and the question raised about the being of the earth are vital acts that are no less genuine, no less man's own. All this happens in every man's solitude. No one

else intervenes in my anguish or in my questioning preoccupation with the being of the thing that disturbs me.
But note that after asking ourselves that question, in the
fundamental solitude which is every man's life, the first
reply that man seeks is not within himself; he is not busy
asking himself the question, but he tends to find it ready-
made in his social environment. After asking himself, he
asks other men; that is to say, he asks out of his own
memory, where he keeps the ideas received from his surroundings, ideas that have been tossed about in school, in
conversation, in reading. He does not, then, seek to find
out for himself what the thing is, but he is first content
with finding out 'what is said' about it. The subject of
this saying is what we called 'people'; the social environment, the collective personage, without individuality,
which is no definite person and is, therefore, irresponsi-
ble. Note the change which this implies. The anguish and
the first question which this sparks are mine; I live them,
and I am them, on my own account. But now I admit
within myself as a reply an idea which is not mine, an
idea that I did not create but took out of the atmosphere.
In short, I supplant my individual 'I' with the social 'I'; I
cease to live my genuine life and make this conform to a
mold that is common, anonymous, ownerless. From
being individual, I move to become communal; in the
realm of thought, I practice vital commonalty.

   Let us make specific some of those elements that are
implied in this change, in that almost instinctive resort of
the genuine 'I' to the unauthentic social 'I' unauthentic,
because whether I like it or not, I am not the others, not
'the people'. 'The people' is not an effective and responsible 'I'. 'The people', the social 'I', is not born and does
not die, does not suffer, does not have to decide its being,
does not think for itself but only *repeats* thoughts; that
is, it 'says' and it talks only in the sense in which saying
and talking are not the same thing as thinking and as tak-

ing account of what is said and what is spoken. For all these reasons, I describe the social 'I' as unauthentic. The common 'I' is no specific and definite 'I'; therefore, it is nobody.

The most interesting elements, I repeat, which are implicit in this shift from my personal 'I' to the social 'I', in the descent from my own self to the collectivity, are as follows:

(1) The lack of confidence in my social surroundings tends to be quieted in my apparent confidence in 'the people'. I distrust nature and trust humanity, society.

(2) This confidence implies, on my part, the belief that there is always a repertory of replies in my social surroundings; for example, that I do not know what the earth is, but 'people' know.

(3) This, in turn, means that man, in living, recognizes that he is always in an atmosphere, or a world, which is not only natural—made up of bodies that are animal, vegetable, mineral—but that, at the same time, he is always afloat in a pre-existent 'culture'. Culture is that ambient repertory of replies to the uneasiness of the genuine or individual life.

(4) Whatever the motives, whether they be well or badly founded, I tend to abandon my own life, to make myself no longer responsible for it, to supplant my own 'I' with a common and unauthentic 'I'.

(5) I admit this response to the people—the vulgar, the common—in one of two ways: either I admit it, rethinking it entirely, and, if so, I do not receive it but I recreate it with my own personal effort, giving it a rebirth out of my own evidence, or I admit it without revising it, without thinking it through; therefore, I admit it *for the very reason* that I do not think it but because 'people' think it, *because* it is said. The phenomenon of abandonment to the social 'I', of not carrying and sustaining oneself but of falling as onto a cushion toward the

convenience of 'it is said', of 'people', of 'public opinion', of the masses which we are now analyzing, is what happens in this last case.

But then note this:

(6) There is a great lack of congruence between the question and the reply. The question, 'What is the earth?', I have thought and have felt in all its moving and inevitable anguish; but the reply, 'the earth is a planet' or something similar, this I neither thought nor rethought, but with this reply I repeat what 'is said', and with this repetition I enter into and become part of 'the people', which is nobody. I, then, turn into nobody, which is what Ulysses, punning with his name, did when he wanted to hide or to disappear.

(7) With this, the cycle of this primary process is closed. I pose the question in view of which the customary earth turned me into a nonbeing, made me a nothing; but in going back to 'what is said' I go back to nobody.

These are the principal implications which the move we make carries within itself whenever we become aware of the antagonism of the environment toward ourselves. This is not a matter here of making history, of what human life is in one period that makes it differ from human life in another period. On the contrary, we are trying to sketch the permanent structure of life, what it always is. In all periods, there functions the system of essential actions of which life consists; the differences between some of them and others proceed from the different proportions of kinds of action and the preponderance of one kind over another. Thus, at certain times, this resorting to the surrounding culture, topical and ready-made, is not stabilized or is less stabilized than at other times. In some periods, man dominates that tendency to abandon himself to the collective and goes back to himself, destroys the surrounding idea, and seeks to make for himself a highly individual opinion of his own. At other times, the opposite occurs. For a philosophy of history, this is a subject of the greatest importance. As we have no intention of going into this discipline now, we will avoid developing it.

Only in passing, and with a sidewise glance, it might be well to leave a hint that as we go back in the chronology of history toward primitive life, this abandoning of one's own life in favor of the social and collective life becomes more marked. In short, the old, established opinion, 'what is said', completely dominates individual thought. There is no one who discriminates, judges, and passes sentence —according to his personal criterion of intimate evidence —on the truth or error of the traditional idea; but on the contrary, the individual submits his spontaneous conviction to the tribunal of tradition. When a thought before me bases its truth on what seems evident to me, the principle which moves me to adapt it is called *reason*. When, on the contrary, it bases its 'truth' on 'what is said' by people since time immemorial, hence, on the crude fact of its repetition, the principle that moves me to adopt it is called *tradition*. Here, reason appears to us as an imperative of each man's reversion to himself. Tradition, on the other hand, appears as an imperative to put aside our 'I myself', melding it into the collective.

If primitive life is characterized by the almost fundamental predominance of the traditional imperative, it is illusory to think that this ceases to act in any period whatsoever. He who is most resolved to follow only reason—that is to say, his own inmost evidence—cannot, in fact, follow this norm except in small sectors of his life; the rest of it he entrusts to tradition and lives on it. Without this sector of conventional ideas he could not live; his lack of security with regard to the greater part of his surroundings would be intolerable. Society, which is to say, tradition, carries him in its arms and, at the same time, keeps him prisoner.

Putting the same thing in another form, we have this:

our own 'I' must exist, whether or not it is boxed within a social 'I', in a tradition, in a world of ideas which are not its own, with which it finds itself and in which it must lodge its own exactly as happens to it with the physical world.

Thus, each age seems to us as a specific equation between reason and tradition, between the genuine life of individuals and the conventional, traditional, communal life.

Equipped with considerations like this, let us turn to our own principal affair. When we asked ourselves, anguished, 'What is the world?', tradition gave us automatically a tangle of ready-made replies, one of which, for the moment, we held onto. Those replies are of different degrees of density; one of them is what the most advanced science thinks in this particular historical moment. Recently born, still fresh from the individual mind of its creator, this reply has not yet succeeded in making its way into the anonymous breadth of the social 'I'. It is still difficult to understand, is still being discussed, has not yet become a mental habit. In order to receive it, one must make no small effort; and it almost obliges us to rethink it on our own account. For these reasons, it does not pacify us at all; it does not seem to us to be the very reality that we seek but to be just another theory, another man's idea. It is the germ of a possible tradition, of a topic which has not yet hardened or been consolidated.

But behind this idea lie other older ones, put forth by the science of yesterday or the day before. These seem to us more like reality itself; they are more satisfactory. But behind these lie still others which seem the primogenitive theories of humanity, decanted into language. And these are completely satisfactory to us. They do not seem to us to be theories; we do not see them as ideas but as effective reality itself. Therefore, it does not occur to us to doubt them. It is relatively easy to become aware that the sky of Copernicus is not a reality but an idea, a human interpretation of reality. It is easy because this is relatively recent and the opposite of what our eyes seem to tell us. But if it said that the sun is a body, this seems to us to coincide so perfectly with reality itself that we do not suspect it of being a theory, an interpretation. Yet the idea of a body assumes an entire conception of the physical world, although a very elemental one, and so old in the human mind that it has been converted into a deep habit on which we rest.

The very idea of a 'thing' sums up a complete metaphysics. Up to this point we have, in defining life, said that man found himself amid things. Now we must state that 'thing' is an interpretation of what was facing man and with which he had to make do. 'Thing' is something to which we attribute permanence in certain characteristics amid their variations, for example, their variations of place. That the sun in the East and the sun in the West is the same sun, that it is the same entity or solid thing, invariable in its main structure and differing in the place in which it is found now and then—this is a bit of wisdom to which man came by force of thinking about his surroundings.

All this acts to make us recognize a most simple truth: that if we strip the worldly environment in which we live of everything we have thought about it and of all the information we have received about it, we will have emptied it completely of being and will have left in its place a tangle of irritating questions.

Now it will be abundantly clear that if our life consists of 'being in a room', this does not mean that it consists in the 'I' which is each of us being in a space. Space is a theory, an idea.

'To be in', used as a concept expressive of the primary reality which is our life, means simply to 'make do with them' to use, to manage, this or that, to 'help oneself with them'. The room in which we now find ourselves living is not even a 'thing'; it is that of which you are making use in order to do whatever you decided to do, which is 'to listen to a lecture'. The room is there; it will be there whether or not we are in it and regardless of what we think about it and how we interpret it. It is adequately adapted to the plan of holding listeners at a lecture, which is the reason you came into it. Therefore, it is not questioned, but you use it without more ado: we would say, you live it as such a room. If there were too many echoes in it, or if sleet should fall on us through holes in the ceiling, we would cease talking about and listening to philosophy and would busy ourselves with this room, and then we would think about what a room is when it is not a room, a lecture hall, a something that serves for listening in.

Lesson IX

*The two tables: the substantial thing and the space
populated by fields of force. The first table is neither the
one nor the other. The game of being.*

'*I have settled down to the task of writing these lectures
and have drawn up my chairs to my two tables. Two tables!
Yes; there are duplicates of every object about me—two
tables, two chairs, two pens* [1].

'*This is not a very profound beginning to a course which
ought to reach transcendent levels of scientific philosophy.
But we cannot touch bedrock immediately; we must scratch
a bit at the surface of things first. And whenever I begin to
scratch the first thing I strike is— my two tables.*

'*One of them has been familiar to me from earliest years.
It is a commonplace object of that environment which I call
the world. How shall I describe it? It has extension; it is
comparatively permanent; it is coloured; above all it is*
substantial. *By substantial I do not merely mean that it does
not collapse when I lean upon it; I mean that it is constituted of "substance" and by that word I am trying to convey
to you some conception of its intrinsic nature. It is a* thing;
*not like space, which is a mere negation; nor like time, which
is—Heaven knows what! But that will not help you to my
meaning because it is the distinctive characteristic of a
"thing" to have this substantiality, and I do not think sub-*

1. This text is made up of paragraphs of the book, *The Nature of
the Physical World* (1929) by Sir A. S. Eddington, Cambridge
University Press, London, which were read and commented on
by Ortega in the course of this lecture. We use the Spanish translation published by the Magazine *SUR*, of Buenos Aires, in 1938
[*Compilers' note*]. [The English text herewith is taken from the
edition issued by The University of Michigan Press in 1958 and
is used here with the permission of Cambridge University Press—
Translator's note.]

stantiality can be described better than by saying that it is the kind of nature exemplified by an ordinary table. And so we go round in circles. After all if you are a plain commonsense man, not too much worried with scientific scruples, you will be confident that you understand the nature of an ordinary table. I have even heard of plain men who had the idea that they could better understand the mystery of their own nature if scientists would discover a way of explaining it in terms of the easily comprehensible nature of a table.

'Table No. 2 is my scientific table. It is a more recent acquaintance and I do not feel so familiar with it. It does not belong to the world previously mentioned—that world which spontaneously appears around me when I open my eyes, though how much of it is objective and how much subjective I do not here consider. It is part of a world which in more devious ways has forced itself on my attention. My scientific table is mostly emptiness. Sparsely scattered in that emptiness are numerous electric charges rushing about with great speed; but their combined bulk amounts to less than a billionth of the bulk of the table itself. Notwithstanding its strange construction it turns out to be an entirely efficient table. It supports my writing paper as satisfactorily as table No. 1; for when I lay the paper on it the little electric particles with their headlong speed keep on hitting the underside, so that the paper is maintained in shuttlecock fashion at a nearly steady level. If I lean upon this table I shall not go through; or, to be strictly accurate, the chance of my scientific elbow going through my scientific table is so excessively small that it can be neglected in practical life. Reviewing their properties one by one, there seems to be nothing to choose between the two tables for ordinary purposes; but when abnormal circumstances befall, then my scientific table shows to advantage. If the house catches fire my scientific table will dissolve quite naturally into scientific smoke, whereas my familiar table undergoes a metamorphosis of its substantial nature which I can only regard as miraculous.

'There is nothing substantial about my second table. It is nearly all empty space—space pervaded, it is true, by fields of force, but these are assigned to the category of "influences", not of "things". Even in the minute part which is not empty we must not transfer the old notion of substance.

In dissecting matter into electric charges we have travelled far from that picture of it which first gave rise to the conception of substance, and the meaning of that conception—if it ever had any—has been lost by the way. The whole trend of modern scientific views is to break down the separate categories of "things", "influences", "forms", etc., and to substitute a common background of all experience. Whether we are studying a material object, a magnetic field, a geometrical figure, or a duration of time, our scientific information is summed up in measures; neither the apparatus of measurement nor the mode of using it suggests that there is anything essentially different in these problems. The measures themselves afford no ground for a classification by categories. We feel it necessary to concede some background to the measures—an external world; but the attributes of this world, except in so far as they are reflected in the measures, are outside scientific scrutiny. Science has at last revolted against attaching the exact knowledge contained in these measurements to a traditional picture-gallery of conceptions which convey no authentic information of the background and obtrude irrelevancies into the scheme of knowledge.

'I will not here stress further the non-substantiality of electrons, since it is scarcely necessary to the present line of thought. Conceive them as substantially as you will, there is a vast difference between my scientific table with its substance (if any) thinly scattered in specks in a region mostly empty and the table of everyday conception which we regard as the type of solid reality—an incarnate protest against Berkleian subjectivism. It makes all the difference in the world whether the paper before me is poised as it were on a swarm of flies and sustained in shuttlecock fashion by a series of tiny blows from the swarm underneath, or whether it is supported because there is substance below it, it being the intrinsic nature of substance to occupy space to the exclusion of other substance; all the difference in conception at least, but no difference to my practical task of writing on the paper.

. . 'I need not tell you that modern physics has by delicate test and remorseless logic assured me that my second scientific table is the only one which is really there—wherever "there" may be. On the other hand I need not tell you that

*modern physics will never succeed in exorcising that first
table—strange compound of external nature, mental imagery
and inherited prejudice—which lies visible to my eyes and
tangible to my grasp. We must bid good-bye to it for the
present for we are about to turn from the familiar world to
the scientific world revealed by physics. This is, or is intended
to be, a wholly external world.'*

AND NOW I ASK—reading Eddington—when I say that I
approach the table in order to write, can that action and
that situation in my life expressed by those words consist
in my approaching some electron? A savage also can approach the table (though he cannot write) in order to sit
on it, and that savage—is he too approaching those electrons?

But the same thing is valid for the table as substance.
Strictly speaking, the first table is neither electrons nor
substance, nor anything else. In itself, it has no being; it
is there as an element in my life, making it easy or difficult. It serves me or does me disservice; it favors me or it
annoys me.

But it might be said that the being of this table is its
being convenient for me. And what if I flee because of
sudden fire? The table gets in my way. Even that being
—being convenient, being difficult—is not the being of
the table, but depends on what I have to do—to write or
to flee.

Therefore, the circumstances, the surroundings—for
the moment and as such—have no being. That mimimum
which they might have is not theirs, but mine. It depends
on what I am—the one who writes or the one who has to
run.

This transfers the problem of the being of things to
me. In order to answer the question, 'What are things?', I
must answer my own question, 'What am I?'.

But I am he who must cope with my surroundings,
who must be in them. What I can be and what I must be
depends, then, in turn, on my environment.

Man and his circumstance, his surroundings, play the

problem of being back and forth—the one tosses it back to the other—which indicates that the problem of being is the problem of each of them, of man and his circumstance, of the whole.

The basic and irremediable fact with which man, in living, finds himself is that neither he nor things have a being; hence, he has no choice but to do something in order to live and to decide from moment to moment what he is going to do; or, what is the same thing, he must decide on his being, and this, as we have seen, includes the being of things.

But 'world' signifies a unitary order of things; it is the being of this order and this and all the things articulated into a universal being. A world is order, structure, law, and definite behavior of things; absolute variation would not be a world[2].

The possible and the impossible.

World is orientation.

Man is disoriented.

Pseudo-orientation in the topic.

But even that topic, before being a topic, was the work of man.

There is no collective work. 'The people' do not do or make anything.

That man had to create—within his own authenticity —the orientation which that concept represents.

Partial orientations, or the question about the being of these or of other things; the sciences.

But the sciences live in a state of disorientation. The number, the mineral, the animal.

Fundamental or universal orientation. The question about the being of being. Metaphysics.

Your life—to be here now. Why?

Life is an interpretation of itself, a justification of itself.

2. In the next section, this last part of the lesson, the manuscript consists of the abbreviations which are transcribed here [*Compilers' note*].

Lesson X

*Our road toward metaphysics. Knowing as 'knowing
what to hold on to'. Construction of the world in the
face of problematical surroundings. Metaphysics is
a task that is inevitable. Metaphysics is solitude.*

IN PREVIOUS LESSONS, we have not even given metaphysics
a name. It might be said that as far as metaphysics is concerned, all we have done is lose time. Today, however,
we are going to mention metaphysics again but this time
rather formally, because we will start in a manner and
with a set of words that are carefully thought out. On
beginning the task, we may perhaps take account of the
fact that previous lessons have given us, unpremeditat-
edly, no small number of bits and pieces of it.

But, in accordance with our usage, let us summarize in
final form what we have been saying.

Our lives are now a matter of being here in this room,
occupied with metaphysics. This is what we are doing.
Life is always a matter of having to do something in
view of the environment in which we find ourselves, of
having to occupy ourselves with something. But this
obligation, this occupation, which, from moment to moment, is our lives, is not given to us as a thing already decided; we must decide it ourselves. In order to decide it,
we need to make for ourselves a question about it; that is,
we need to preoccupy ourselves with that work, that
doing, that occupation, with what we are going to do in
life, with what we are going to be. Hence, all our occupations assume and are born out of one essential occupation; the matter of occupying ourselves with our own
being. But, for the moment, our being consists of having

118

to be here in our environment. Hence, the occupation with our own being, the making a question about it, carries with it the making a question about that which surrounds and envelopes us. We ask ourselves, 'What is this table on which I am leaning? What is this light that illumines me?'. And also, 'What am I? Am I he who uses the table, who is in the room, the one on whom this light shines?'.

Why do we ask ourselves these questions? Because, when I find myself living, what I find consists of the fact that I must be I, not within myself, but outside myself, amid all that surrounds me, and these surroundings surge up at me like something other than myself, like an element that resists me, that denies and refuses me. That 'I, being myself, here' does not go ahead by itself, but that living is precisely having to make it, having to achieve it. The 'I, being here', which is life, I find as a task, as a problem that I need to solve. I must, then, take hold of it with the 'here' and the 'with myself'. For this, I need to organize my doing, and in order to organize it, I need to orient myself in the 'here', in my surroundings. If I don't, I cannot take a single step. Why am I going to do better in one direction than in another? Even more, why, why, am I going to take a step? Why not renounce all doing and let myself die? But even if I resolve to let myself die, I must rationalize my resolution, must be oriented about my life; only thus will such a decision 'have meaning'. It assumes my having convinced myself that it is better to die than to live. But this, in turn, implies that I am perfectly oriented about life, that is, that I know what life is and everything in it.

One cannot live without some interpretation of life. This is a strange reality which carries within itself its own interpretation. This interpretation is, at the same time, a justification. Whether I like it or not, I must justify to myself every one of my acts. Human life is, then, at once crime, criminal, and judge.

So it is impossible for man to be without orientation when he faces the problem that is his life. For the very reason that life is, at root, always disorientation, perplexity, not knowing what to do, it is also an attempt to orient itself, to know what things are and what man in the midst of them is. Because he must deal with them, he needs to know what to depend on with respect to them. The term 'to know' means just that—to know what to look for, to cling to, to depend on with respect to something, to know what has to be done with it or in view of it.

I am oriented with respect to something when I possess a plan of my dealings with it, of my action in regard to it, and that plan of my behavior assumes that I have made a plan of this thing, a figure or a sketch of what this thing represents in my life. That figure, or that sketch, is the being of the other things and as the being of this thing links me completely with the being of others I do not manage to obtain it; I cannot orient myself basically with respect to it unless I have oriented myself with respect to everything else, unless I have made a plan of all of them. That plan of all these things is the world or universe, and the fundamental orientation which it provides is metaphysics.

(The mathematician is oriented with respect to numbers and figures; but only in part, for the reason that he is not oriented with respect to the relationship of both with everything else.)

This discovery puts us up against something unexpected: that metaphysics, or man's fundamental orientation, is not something that is adventitious, something that some men called philosophers do from time to time, but that they very well might not do; it is not something, therefore, that the rest of mankind does not, perforce, have to do. On the contrary, we find that metaphysical activity is an inevitable ingredient of human life; even more, that it is what man is always doing, and all his other occupations are decantings precipitated from it. In short, when you think that in coming to a class in metaphysics you are doing something new, perhaps interesting, perhaps superfluous, you find that throughout your whole life you have been doing nothing else. In fact, you have done whatever you have done in view of a certain interpretation of the circumstances surrounding you in every case. Most of that interpretation came to you from the social circle in which you found yourselves; but you had to receive it, to assimilate it, to adhere to it, and, more often than you think, you have made your choice among the different ideas about the world and the things of the world which your circle offered you. You have, then, made metaphysics.

Metaphysics is not a science; it is a construction of the world, and this making a world out of what surrounds you is human life. The world, the universe, is not given to man; what is given to him is his circumstances, his surroundings, with their numberless contents. But this circumstance and everything in it is, in itself, pure problem. Now, one cannot *be present* in a pure problem. The pure problem is like the earthquake or the sea, something in which one *cannot be*. We are not standing in an earthquake; we are falling. In the sea, we are sinking. The pure problem is the absolute insecurity which obliges us to make for ourselves a form of security. What saves us is the interpretation which we give to our circumstance, our surroundings, and in the measure in which it convinces us, we believe in it, and it makes us secure. And as the world (or the universe) is no more than that interpretation, we will hold that the world is the security in which man succeeds in being. The world is that in which we are secure.

So we arrive at this statement: human life is not being what it already is, but it is the having to be, having to act in order to be; therefore, it is not yet being. The most immediate expression of this is found by noting that what

most concerns us is whether or not we will continue to
be in the very next moment. The present is no longer important to us. Hence, the fundamental substance of life
would be insecurity. But by the same token, it is at the
same time an impulse, a desire for security, and the construction of the world which makes security possible.
Man makes his world in order to install himself in it, to
save himself in it; man is metaphysics. Metaphysics is a
thing that is inevitable.

Now we will, for you and for me, consider how man
may be good metaphysics.

Having reached this point, we have only to proceed
with a bit of order. We said that metaphysics is a basic
orientation; let us think a bit about the conditions of a
basic orientation.

To be basic, we cannot limit the area of life in which
we are about to orient ourselves. The physicist is oriented in regard to corporeal things; everything else is
outside his sphere, and the rest does not concern him. As
long as he is able to know what to find out about bodies,
all the rest stays intact for him. If there is, in addition to
bodies, another kind of reality, how does this concern
him? It does not even matter to him what the value and
the place of corporeal reality in the universe might be.
Hence, he accepts the world without making a question
out of it; that is, he takes the rest of the world as tradition and his social surroundings think it is. Or, to put it
another way, the physicist, on making for himself a problem concerning the being of bodies, cannot accept any
opinion about bodies without previous examination and
proof; but he freely accepts as dependably solid any
other sector of opinion which does not deal with bodies.
For example, he accepts mathematics, takes it as true,
and, trusting it, he uses it in his laboratory. He accepts
the laws of logic, he accepts—without discussion—the
apparent fact that man is capable of science, and so on.
All this he can do because he does not pretend to a basic
orientation.

In contrast, we now see what is characteristic of this basic type of orientation—the refusal to accept any opinion if we cannot answer for its firmness and, therefore, the refusal to accept as certain any opinion for which we ourselves cannot answer.

Note what this carries with it. The physicist can take advantage of certain outside opinions, valuing them for himself as long as they are useful to him. He builds his science by depending on the convictions of others who are not physicists. So he makes his science with the aid of others. But the metaphysician, having to renounce every opinion which he himself does not fabricate, being unable to accept from others any opinion as good and firm, must make it all himself, or, what is the same thing, he has to remain alone. Metaphysics is solitude. Others can put us on the road to it, but when we truly make metaphysics, that is, when we fabricate our own basic convictions, we must build each one by itself and for itself, in fundamental solitude. No one, no matter how excellent his intentions, can hand us our convictions ready-made. It is we ourselves who must *convince ourselves.*

The statement in which we express a conviction of ours about the being of something is called a thesis, or a position, or a proposition; the name is significant enough. If we have, in fact, come to be convinced of something, that something stays firm and in place for us.

Well now, our *theses* are of two kinds: on the one hand, all those of which we are convinced because they are supported by others that are also solid; and on the other hand, the primary *theses* of which solidity is not a matter of stemming from any previous theses.

Here, you have the essential difficulty inherent in a basic orientation; that it needs to start from certain primary theses which do not base their truths or their solidity on others, and yet, nevertheless, do affirm themselves to themselves. All the rest are supported on these, depend on them, take from them their own security.

Lesson XI

*A first conviction about the whole. What is it that
there truly is? First thesis: things and their entirety, or the
world; their attributes. Second thesis: idealism; ingenuousness
and caution.*

LOST IN OUR OWN LIFE—life is the feeling of being lost—
we seek a basic orientation in respect to it. To orient
oneself presupposes pure multiplicity, the existence before our eyes of many things of which we know only
that we do not know what they are; we neither know
them one by one, nor in their relationship with others,
nor in their existence as a group. In short, the process of
orientation presupposes chaos.

The first act in a basic orientation must consist of obtaining a first certainty about this chaos, what is usually
called a first conviction. The content of the first conviction is the first truth. We want to know on what we can
depend in regard to things, and now we are deciding on
our first assumptions. Being the first, this means that we
are going to rest on it or to found on it all the other assumptions—otherwise, it would not be first except in
chronology. It would be a conviction which I now
achieve, after which there will follow another that has
nothing to do with the first, and so on, successively. If I
proceed in this fashion, I will find myself with a horde of
unconnected convictions; therefore, in wishing to orient
myself amid the chaos of my surroundings, I find myself
newly lost in the chaos of my convictions. So, I do not
need mere convictions as such, but a system of convictions, that is, a limited group of them in which some
would be connected. This assumes that the first convic-

tion would be of such a kind that I could let myself lean on it in order to obtain the rest. If not, I would spend my life beginning and never arriving at a finite and limited group of convictions, of truths or *theses*.

So I must start with a thesis that gives me a first certainty, that is, that tells me or shows me something about my entire situation which is certain. The first thesis, then, must be universal. But in addition, as it is the first, it must be sure of itself, and, therefore, it cannot assume an earlier one on whose certainty it can rest. For this, it is necessary that it be not implicated in or complicated with another of the same range.

My life is whatever *there is*, whatever I find in it, and my question with respect to this 'whatever there is' is this: 'How much should I pay heed, intellectually, to whatever there is?'; that is, what ought I to think, for the moment, about whatever there is? *What I ought to think* about anything, the appropriate thought or my correct intellectual behavior about something; this is the *being* of that something. Hence, my first question leading toward a basic orientation is not 'What is there?', but 'What is what-is-there?'. The former I already have, because living is being in the midst of things, making do with them; of course I have them, of course they are there, and, therefore, I am lost amongst them. What is asked is not, then, *what there is*, but *what is* what-there-is, what is the way of being of this what-there-is. It does not matter if we express the same thing inversely, saying, 'What *being* is there?'. Here, the 'is there' refers not to things but to 'being'. In the chaos in which I am—and which I am— there are innumerable elements, faces, forms; it is a chaos for the very reason that *there are* so many ingredients. I need to decide which, among all these faces, elements, forms, and ways, is the fundamental one, the one to which all others can be reduced and from which all the rest are mere derivation, resultant, or combination. That is to say, among all there is, there is something which is the truth of all the rest; therefore, it is this which is what there *truly* is.

So that you may understand me, I will cite a partial example. The physicist tells me that when colors and luminous bodies appear before me, what is really there is aetherial vibration or an electromagnetic field. Of course, he does not deny that there is also light which I see such and as I see it, but he invites me to recognize that that light and those colors are there thanks to the fact that there is an electromagnetic field or that there is ether. There is, then, light and there is a field, but these two instances of 'there is' stand in an hierarchical relationship and do not mean the same thing to me; the field is a primary presence, and the fact that there are colors stands as a consequence or secondary derivative of the field.

We frequently dream, and it is beyond question that there is the thing which is dreamed; but it is also beyond question that the dreamed thing is not a 'there is' in the same sense as what we see when we are awake. This latter is a matter of reality; that is, it has a greater degree of reality than has the dreamed thing. The object of which I dream is a reality, but the object that I see when awake and from which the dreamed thing stems has, with respect to the latter, a primary, originating, or fundamental reality.

Our first thesis of orientation concerning what there is seeks, then, the basic reality of how much there is, what there really is, or the being of what there is. In view of this, we must make our terminology precise and understand by reality only that which is fundamental; there is the rest, but not in reality; rather in appearance or derivatively.

If we do not begin by assuring ourselves of reality, which is like a cellar floor on which all the rest is based and of which all the rest is a mere aspect, a transformation, or a consequence, we will continue to be lost.

In this way, we state as a first thesis the same thing that

occupies first place, chronologically speaking, in the history of philosophy; it is this—reality, or being, consists of things and their aggregate which we call the world.

Do not think that world, as used here, means the same as it did in earlier lessons or other lectures and thus try to anticipate what I am going to say. You probably remember that it cost you a bit of effort to understand this new meaning which I was giving to the term 'world' as an interpretation of circumstance, of surroundings, as a system of our convictions. This difficulty arose out of the fact that you were then in the midst of the fundamental thesis which we are now presenting, which, for reasons we will see, is the natural thesis, that is, the first and most obvious thesis for man.

Things are what is already here, without my seeking them and before I seek them. The aggregate of things is the world. This world is here and I am in it; I am a piece of it, a thing of the world.

The world, or reality, or what truly is, then, is presented to us as the great thing. Its manner of being, its type of reality, is before us, is that which is offered to us before any one of those objects that we call things.

This thesis which, I repeat, is the initial and most obvious one, the first in human history, and the first in the reaction of the individual mind, meets the characteristics or attributes of being in the thing. And by 'thing' we understand, first of all, what we see and touch, what we find to be our surroundings that are subject to our senses.

This thesis, let me say again, goes like this: What there truly is, reality, what is, is the world.

Let us understand what we have thought in these words—and, therefore, which are the attributes that constitute this way of being.

A thing is first, something that I encounter, something which, therefore, is there by itself, independent of me. The *being* of that wall is, for the moment, to stand there on its own account. Second, the being of what is there, insofar as it is *already* there, is a fixed and finished being, a being that is already what it is. This wall consists of a definite color, is in a fixed form. In short, the being of the thing is already a being, a quiet, static being, being what it is.

The second point we are going to leave for the moment untouched; we still have too much to do with the first; reality as the world, as that which is there by itself, and of which I am no more than a single piece. In the final instance, in reality, I am—with some variations—as the stone is, something that is there; 'there' meaning in the mass of things. To be there is to be forming a part of the world.

This thesis well defines a certain manner of being which is that of what are called 'things', and as these are undoubtedly something-there-is, it defines the being of something there undoubtedly is. But it is not said that 'things' are the most basic objects, and that everything there is can be reduced to that manner of being. This thesis means raising to the status of prototype of all being the peculiar manner of being which pertains to the 'thing', the *res;* and for this reason it is called realism. Realism, then consists of the thesis, or affirmation, that everything that is, is by definition as the thing is.

Such an affirmation has one characteristic that renders it, in effect, worthy of being a first thesis; this is its universality. It is the taking of an intellectual position with respect to how much there is. But now we need to ask ourselves if it fulfills the other essential condition of a first thesis, namely, is it sure of itself, is it beyond any doubt?

In order that this be certain, it must neither implicate nor complicate another thesis of its same range.

Now, what does 'world' mean? That which is there, by itself; for example, this wall, this room in which I am. Very well; but if I am going out of this room, does the room with its wall continue to be here? Evidently, because I call 'something being here', a being here on its own account, independent of me. This is precisely what I understand by 'thing'; and by 'world', that which is independent of me. (What is dreamed is dreamed by me, it depends on some sense of mine; if there is no dreamer, there is nothing dreamed.) Being is the same as being in and by itself, and not for me.

Of course! But I insist: If I leave this room, which I have described as being here by itself, which is a *reality*, logic (which underlies my concepts) impels me, on pain of contradiction, to state that this room will continue to be here. But this consequence to which logic impels me also opens my eyes to the error lying beneath my initial thesis, because it is evident that if I find myself far from this room, I can no longer be certain that it is here. When I close my eyes that wall disappears, it ceases to be here. Therefore, my assertion that the wall and the room are here on their own account, by themselves, was not so solid. In the 'being here' of things, I myself intervene. They are here insofar as I see them, touch them, think them. Only then does their 'being here' become sure and beyond doubt.

It is, of course, very probable that this room would continue to be here when I go out of it; but a thesis of basic orientation and, above all, one that is the first and will be decisive for all the rest, does not admit of probabilities. It must be entirely sure and solid. The theses that are probable and unsure were those that I had in my life before solving for myself the matter of basic orientation, and because they were of that type, I felt lost in chaos. Now, it is a matter of obtaining complete security and of putting one's foot down on land that is entirely firm and solid; we need what I called in Platonic terms—when I was twenty-odd and wrote *Meditations on Quixote*—the 'certainty of the position', τό ἀσφαλές της ὑπόδεσεως [1].

1. *Phaedo*, 100 d, 101 d [*Compilers' note*].

In short, the thesis that affirms that reality is the world, is things, has as a result the complicating of another—that reality is a subject that thinks the world, that thinks things.

The reality of this wall is problematical; the reality of my vision of this wall is indubitable. This, then, the reality of my thoughts, my ideas, is the firm and solid reality. The realist thesis is annulled, leaving in its place the idealist thesis. Historically, this happened in the time of Descartes. It is the modern thesis. On it, as on firm ground, Western man has lived—with certain modulations—from 1600 up to our own days. The interpretation of life and, therefore, of man and of the world, in which we have been brought up, which is absorbed within us, which we met when we were born, and which, in consequence, held our world together, was the idealist interpretation. (Frenchmen, Englishmen, Germans, the seventeenth century, eighteenth century, nineteenth century —idealism! The twentieth century begins: in 1900 comes the *Logical Investigations* of Husserl; in 1913, his *Ideas for a Pure Phenomenology*—the most extreme, most rigorous form of idealism.) This, then, is the thesis within which we find ourselves. We live in a world that has been forged by idealism. The question is whether we can continue in that thesis, for everything makes one suspect that it is breaking apart and will go down.

But you understand that the idealist thesis is very hard to shatter. It is always difficult to supersede one basic thesis with another for the very reason that it is basic. But it is much more difficult when this thesis has already pushed aside another initial one. That initial thesis, the realist thesis, imposed itself by being the most natural and obvious one; that was its power, which was not small. It expresses and formulates that which, we might say, is seen at a single glance, that which occurs to us when we let our thinking follow its first inclination. It is not hidden from us how difficult it is to correct a first glance and a natural inclination with a second glance, because this second glance does not blur, erase, or blot out the first, but preserves it and explains it. The Copernican thesis superseded our first idea that the sun moves, which is the most obvious and natural idea; but in superseding it, the Copernican interpretation did not abolish that earlier idea. Your convinced disciple of Copernicus continues to see the sun sinking in the West. The same thing is true of the idealist. He must recognize realism as a partial truth. So his problem and his peculiar difficulty is to explain how, as thought is the true reality, things seem to have a reality which is independent of that.

The first thesis, given its strength in being the most natural, obvious, and indestructible one, has the weakness of being ingenuous. By this I mean that the realists of Greece and of the Middle Ages were realists without taking particular care to be realists. They were realists in a paradisiacal sense, because it never occurred to them that there was any room for an opposite thesis—So much so that there was no philosophy, strictly speaking, until Descartes came along, that would specifically formulate the thesis on which the realists were living. Because it was the pure and indisputable one, it never occurred to them even to state it much less to prove it. Hence, it would be a thesis which did not have its defense prepared.

Idealism had only to enunciate the realist thesis formally, to have its impossibility demonstrated by the most superficial analysis. Idealism itself is the proof of the impossibility of realism. Idealism was born, then, of a proof, as the result of having lost ingenuousness and of thinking with care and great caution. It is a natively cautious thesis and on the defensive. Hence, the enormous difficulty of attempting to supersede it. It is fortified with sharp points and well armed. To touch it, in order to push it aside, is to expose oneself to dialectic jabbings and to fail in the attempt.

Lesson XII

*The point of departure is insecurity. Which is the
fundamental reality? The realist thesis complicates thought.
Conformity and anticonformity. Thought and its forms.
The idealist thesis does away with the outside world.*

WE STARTED TO WIN a fundamental security, which we
need for the very reason that what is first given to us
when life is given to us is fundamental insecurity.

We need, first, to find a footing for ourselves, to find
something firm amid what there is; and we ask ourselves
what it is that is truly there, what reality is.

And we formulate a first thesis: reality is things and
their utility, or the real world. What is peculiar about
things, what invites us to formulate this thesis affirming
that they are the fundamental reality, is that they are
there in themselves and for themselves. The world of
things is all there is. I am one of those things. I am here in
the midst of them. I am a piece of the world. Such is the
realist thesis—the most obvious one and the first in
human history and in each man, whatever the period in
which he lives.

It would be interesting to sketch the structure given to
life by finding oneself holding the conviction which
makes it and one's life a thing that is in the world; or,
what is the same thing, that to be a man, and living, is to
be the world. Our earlier lessons have unintentionally
taught us too much without my wanting it, have made us
see that whatever may be the true and definitive thesis
concerning the fundamental reality we seek, our life is
not the world. Because we have seen that to live is for me
to be myself amid my surroundings, or the world, as in

132

an element that is alien to me. The world, then, is only a term in my life; but I am not the world, nor is my life a thing of this world. For this very reason, my life is not there—as are the stone, the tree, and the star—but I must make it for myself, and to me it is pure effort and pure problem.

But now we must forget this for one reason. Up to this point we have done nothing—and note this well—but describe the phenomenon which the word 'life' designates; we have not said a single formal word about the degree of reality which corresponds to that phenomenon. The phenomenon includes everything there is and everything I find. I find the stone, I find this room, I find the centaurs that I imagine, I find geometric triangles, and I find —no more and no less than all this—that which I call my life.

Since what is characteristic of this phenomenon—once I become aware of it—is that my life seems to me like the compass within which all the rest is put, the place where I find it or where it is, I have sometimes urged you to note that this reality which we call our life *seems* to include all the rest. But we said nothing more; we did not formalize this mere appearance and for the reason that we had not, until now, posed for ourselves the limiting and peremptory question, 'Which is the basic, the fundamental, reality?'. Up to now, we were talking only of life. But now, as we ask ourselves this question, we are talking of everything there is; and on facing up to this, we ask ourselves formally—eager to reach a decision— what, of all there is, is *the* reality, that is, the fundamental reality?

Up to now, all has been preparation and nothing else; preparation for entering upon the system of our convictions, or the truth. Now, we are seeking a first truth, the most important, the basic truth, the truth on which all the rest will depend.

And we have proposed to ourselves as the first truth

that realist thesis. That thesis is so obvious, so natural, that it has forever stamped itself in our vocabulary. When we want to say about something that there truly is this thing which is the prototype of being, we call it reality. Now, this word does not properly mean any more than the peculiar manner of being of things, the *res,* the external, the corporeal. Nevertheless, we use the word today to include that which is not *res,* not external or corporeal. He who insists that the fundamental reality is the spirit uses the word without remembering that the manner of being of the spirit is very different from the manner of being of a *res;* for example, of a stone. Note, then, that in this word, two different meanings have become fused and confused—one, the characteristic of that which finally and definitively exists; the other, the peculiar manner of being of external things.

Noting this, we can now return to our initial thesis: reality is made up of things and their grouping, or the world. Things are reality because they are there in and by themselves, put there by themselves, sustaining themselves in existence. As this is the only authentic form of being which that thesis affirms, everything—in the measure in which it is reality—must be like that. For example, man; I myself. My reality also consists in being a thing among things, like a stone, like a plant. Man, then, lives within this thesis, interpreting himself to himself as a thing of the external world; or, what is the same thing, he puts himself from then on in the midst of things, in the landscape. You will come to understand what this means. It is enough now to bring to mind the way we ourselves, even today, see the animal. The monkey hanging from a tree in the forest belongs in this; he has a manner of being which is ultimately identical with that of the tree in which he lives.

Let us now see if this thesis is solid. Being the first one, as we have said several times, it must affirm itself to itself, not founding its truth on the truth of another thesis; or, which is the same thing, it must be indubitable. And, moreover, it must not complicate any other thesis as primitive or primary as it is. Two primary theses would be a contradiction.

Well then, is it beyond doubt that the world of things is there in itself, by and for itself, and, therefore, like the sole reality, independent of anything else? If I should not see things, not touch them, not think that they are there, would things in fact be there? If, making a mental experiment, I subtract myself from the world, does the world remain? Does the reality called 'world' remain? At the very least, this is doubtful; the reality of the world becomes indubitable only when, in addition to its existence, I am there seeing it, touching it, and thinking that it is there. So the certainty of its reality depends on my reality. This, the existence, the reality of a subject that thinks the reality of the world, is what, beyond any doubt, assures the reality of the world. But then the world is not real of itself and in itself, but in and through me. It is real insofar as my thought sets it as real, thinks of it as real. But this reveals that fundamental reality does not belong to it, but is mine. Consequently, the reality of a thing cannot be fundamental, unique, if it is sure only when it is first assured by the reality of the subject that thinks it. In short, the thesis which affirms the reality of the world assumes the thesis which affirms the reality of thought. But the one cancels out the other. Of the world, only one single thing remains as ultimately real—namely, thought; and we have now moved to the second position of man in history, the idealist position.

I said previously that it would be of great interest to outline the structure which the realist convictions give to life; that is, to believe that there is no other reality than the world, and that life, in consequence, is just one thing among other things. Strictly speaking, and though this may seem untrue, that picture of the realist life has never been made in depth. In Husserl, it is described only at its starting point, as what he calls the 'natural thesis'; but he does not even try to describe the consequences of that thesis for the structure of life, that is, how man lives when he is living under the inspiration of and within the conviction of that thesis.

One would have to do something similar with idealism. What shape is given to our lives by the fundamental conviction that the ultimate reality is man's thought? The interesting aspect of this becomes clear merely by comparing the one with the other, the idealist life with the realist life. But we cannot attempt here to sketch the picture of either one—this would take too long.

Think only of the basic inversion which is implicit in the move from one interpretation of life to the other. In realism, to live is to find oneself in a position of security on the firm ground of the world, because the realist world is a world of things that are already there, in themselves, by and for themselves. The realist—and note this well—has his *world* set so that it starts from his belief that it is found there, and nothing more. He will have to go on discovering in detail what kind of a world this is, what are the laws of its behavior and its being. But he knows in advance that those laws are in it and that it has a being.

The idealist, on the other hand, finds himself with the fact that certainty and the world with it have been pulled out from beneath his feet; all that is left as the sole reality is the subject himself. There is, in truth, nothing but his thoughts. Consequently, there is nothing he can lean on because there is nothing outside himself. He must uphold himself, and, like the character in the folk tale, he must get out of the well by pulling himself up by his ears. This man must absolutely make for himself the world in which he is going to live; more than this, living for him is converted into constructing a world, because there is none; instead of learning what the world is by adapting himself to it, as the realist does, he must take the world out of his own head.

For the realist, living will be conforming to the world and, therefore, making himself conform to the world. Realism is conformity. But for the idealist, the problem will be one of creating a world according to our thoughts. It is not enough to conform to what is there, for what is there is not reality; it is necessary to make for oneself what is there—the things that are assumed—so that these are adapted to our ideas which are the authentic reality. Well now, this is the anticonformist spirit, the revolutionary spirit. Idealism is, in essence, revolutionary.

Let this serve, I repeat, as a simple hint of the contradictory structures which the one basic thesis and the other allot to life.

But now we must take a closer look at the idealist thesis.

To affirm that the fundamental reality lies in things—this was an error because the reality of things is certain only as long as a thinking subject is present. Therefore, it is not possible that things are all that exists. If only things existed, we could not be sure of anything; that is, their existence would not be sure, nor would their reality. Only insofar as things are thought of by me am I certain that they exist; but then, that certainty is not so much a certainty of them as it is in my thought of them. The reality of things, then, complicates the reality of thought.

Let us now see if this new thesis is sufficient, or if—by chance—it also complicates another even firmer and more fundamental.

It does not seem that way. That this wall which I see exists when I do not see can be doubted. But it is beyond doubt that it does exist, that my seeing it is real. Considered in and for themselves, things are problematical. On the other hand, considered as thoughts of mine and, hence, set in place by thought, they are entirely firm. They are not there by themselves, but they are in me, in a me which thinks. Thought, then, would be the material out of which everything is made; it would be the only, the unique, basic reality. And as anything else there might be would have to have been previously thought, it remains included by first intent in the thesis which is presented to us as invulnerable, in that it does not seem to complicate any other thesis which is not already included in it.

Objections to the realist thesis are here summed up: that in making it a universal affirmation concerning reality, in tracing the circle or maximum compass of what there truly is, it leaves itself outside. It says that things are what is real, but, for the moment, this is a thought of mine, and while I am thinking the exclusive reality of things, I am in fact adding a different reality—that of the thought with which I think it.

The idealist thesis does not have this inconvenience; it does not leave itself outside. The statement that reality is thought includes itself because it is a thought.

The idealist thesis thus practices an instantaneous conjuring trick, and a transmutation as formidable as these are surprising. Things, everything—this table, that wall, the mountain in the distance, the star—have all been magically converted into thought.

It is, then, well for us to take a good look at what the thing we call thought really is.

Thought is seeing, hearing, imagining, holding concepts. All these are forms of thought. And what all of them have in common is that in them a subject takes account of an object, a subject is conscious of something, or that there is something here for him. Well now, the attributes of a thing are not the same as those in taking account of a thing, of being conscious of it. For example, that wall is white and wide; it is 5 or 6 meters long. But my consciousness, my thought of that wall is neither that it is white nor that it is extensive. Do you see the basic difficulty which this poses for idealism?

When idealism tells me that the firm and sure reality of a thing is that I think it and that, *therefore*, things are my thoughts, we find ourselves facing the fact that we do not know what this means—because the wall is white and 6 meters long, but my thought of the wall, my seeing it or being conscious of it, has nothing white about it, nor has it a millimeter of length. In order that the reality 'wall' can be converted into the thought 'wall', it must, then, cease to be a wall. And if, instead of the wall, we take a more extensive example, for instance, the 'outside', the space in which the wall is, we get this: that when the space becomes thought, it ceases to be spatial and an outside in order to be converted into something unspatial and within me.

Idealism does not, of course, ignore this difficulty; moreover, it takes account of the fact that as the specific difficulty of realism was to be sure that things are as they are in themselves and as they appear to us—that is to say, as they are in our thought—so the specific difficulty of idealism consists in making clear to us how it is that as reality is nothing but unspatial thought, there are nevertheless spatial things—like the body or the external world.

It is important for us to remind ourselves that, according to the idealist thesis, the mind finds itself in two different situations. When I see the wall, and insofar as I see it by myself, the wall exists before me only as a wall, white, and 6 meters long. At that moment, the formula which would best express what there is would be the realist statement: there is a thing which is independent of me, and it is that wall. This would be the exact expression, because insofar as I am seeing the wall, there is, for me, no thought of it, no thought labelled 'my seeing the wall'. My seeing the wall, or thinking it, appears only when I abandon the wall, cease to see it, and, in a new mental act, take account of the fact that I have—a moment earlier—created a vision or a thought of the wall. Only now have I a right to say that there is thought. But on the other hand, now, when I note that what is there is a consciousness or a thought of the wall, there is no longer a wall.

Lesson XIII

We seek a fundamental truth—universal and independent.
The idealist thesis complicates a reality which is different
from thought. The active being of thought and the objective
being of thought. The earlier position of reality. Reality is
my coexistence with things.

WE HAVE NOW REACHED the most serious moment. We
are going to decide on the fundamental principle in the
system of our convictions, the primary truth in the
corpus of our truths. This is the basic truth, and, therefore, it must be rooted, radical. Fundamental, in the universality of its content and also in regard to the independent adequacy of its truth.

The realist thesis, which affirms the existence of the
world of things, seemed in both dimensions to be insuffi-
ciently basic, because in affirming the existence of the
world, it left outside of it this thought in which I make
that affirmation. It is essential that the first thesis include
itself. But, in addition, the affirmation of the existence of
the world is not, in itself, beyond all doubt. Only that
part of the world which is here before me now exists beyond any doubt. The indubitable reality is not, then, the
reality of what is there, but the reality of what stands before me for the very reason that it is here before me. So
the reality of the world assumes my reality. When I
affirm the existence of the world, I have already affirmed
my own existence. I must be present at the thing so that
its existence may be beyond doubt; or, what is the same,
that which is indubitable is not the thing, but its presence
here before me. This presence of the thing before me has
been called thought. Consequently, the indubitable and

primary reality is thought.

We were asking ourselves if this new thesis, the idealist thesis, is firm and solid, that is, whether it is sufficiently fundamental in both dimensions previously described.

For the moment, it seems to be fully universal. Everything to which I can refer will have to be a thought of mine; if not, if I do not think about it, I could not refer myself to it. But, in addition, the statement that reality is the thought does not, as does the realist thesis, leave on the outside this thought in which I make such a statement. This is what gives it the dimension of universality.

Let us now see how the idealist thesis works insofar as the element of indubitability is concerned, that is, in not complicating another thesis, different from it, but one that it needs in order to be true.

This obliges us to pose the question very precisely so that there can be no possible escape from it.

For the effects of the fundamental thesis, we have understood by reality 'that which truly and undoubtedly is'. According to the realist thesis, what truly exists are things, a world; these are what exist in and for themselves, independent of me. This was an error, and we have made the idealist correction: the existence of something completely independent of me is essentially questionable and problematical; consequently, it cannot be a primary truth. The only thing beyond doubt is that what there is, is there in relationship with me, dependent on me, that which *there is for me*. Up to now, the idealist thesis appears to be invulnerable. The being independent of me, which realism ingenuously affirms, cannot be justified. There is only, with undoubted truth, what is there for me.

But now I ask, allowing no evasion or subterfuge, 'What is there when there is only what there is for me?'. At the moment, there is that wall. Idealism then says, therefore, there is not only a wall and nothing more, but there is this 'being a wall for me' and this 'being some-

thing for me' which is called a thought. So idealism con-
cludes that there is only a thought, a subject that thinks
the wall, a subject for which there is a wall. There are
not things, but only the consciousness or the thought of
things.

On reaching this point we must go fearlessly ahead and
force the idealist to make his thesis more precise. To this
end, we ask him, 'What is in the universe when there is
only consciousness, only thought?'. And he replies,
'There is a subject which thinks, or observes, and his action consists only in this; there is this noticing of something, or being conscious of something, or thinking, and,
properly speaking, there is nothing else'. Because the
something that observes, of which he is conscious or
about which he thinks—for example, the wall—is not
truly there but is something inside of thought; and only
in this situation and because of this is it a thing. It means
the same, then, to say that there is only thought or consciousness as to say that there are no things, in that for
them to be now means for the thought of them to be.
This is authentic idealism.

Idealism has always nourished itself on the example of
hallucination, which is most favorable to it. Let us, then,
analyze hallucination. Let us suppose that those of us
who are here suddenly suffer such an ailment; all of a
sudden we see a furious bull rush in. I ask what there is in
the universe while we are in the midst of this hallucination. There is a furious bull; beyond any doubt there is
one, and we are terrified of it. There is the subject as
truly as there is the thing—the bull—and there is no
more the one than the other.

But note that later, for whatever reason, we think that
this was all a matter of hallucination. We have emerged
from the previous moment in which we were seeing a
bull. We are now in a second moment, in which we see
that what happened earlier was an hallucinatory thought.
What is there in the universe while we are engaged in

this second thought? There we are—the subject—and there is the previous hallucinatory thought, though it now seems like a past, a true, effective past, resembling a reality that was, but an absolute reality. What there is not, or ever was, is a bull. From this second instant forward, we cancel out the bull as unreal, we blot out the thing that a moment ago was an absolute reality. The absolute reality for us is an earlier hallucinatory thought, now gone by; this is what there is.

But I ask, 'What meaning for the first instant has this retroactive effect of what happened in the second instant?'. The fact that, on the basis of my present conviction, I describe the earlier one as a mere hallucination does not blot out the situation of the universe, of the reality that was there before. The bull was there, in front of me; there absolutely was a bull, neither more nor less of a bull than there is now only an hallucination, a thought of a bull. I passed through two successive convictions, but as convictions they were identical; both of them enjoyed what is inexorable in convictions, namely, that its subject, the thing of which we are convinced, is absolutely there. Now that I am convinced that I suffered an hallucination, who will assure me that it was not there while I was actually suffering it? While the hallucination is in force, it does not exist for me. And as the idealist thesis consists precisely in affirming that there is only what there is for me, there is no such thing as the thought that I think because while I am thinking it, that thought does not exist for me. It is necessary that I cease to hold it in force, cease to be thinking it, and out of another new one, it is converted into an object for me.

But it will be said that on remembering that earlier thought now and what that object was for me, in the last analysis, it exists for me. Not at all—and the proof of this is that the universe has changed from then to now. Then, when I was thinking my first thought, there absolutely

was in the universe, here, a furious bull. Now there is
nothing but a thought about a furious bull; a thought
about a bull is not a horned animal. Now there is in front
of me only 'somebody'—my earlier 'I'—that thought he
was seeing a bull. It is not possible that this 'object-
thought' and that 'thought-in-action' are the same, given
the fact that its consequences in terms of reality are so
different. They would be the same only if now, on describing the earlier situation, I should take it as it then
appeared and say, 'earlier, I really saw a most real bull'.
But then there would be no idealism; it would not be true
that there is only thought.

So it is necessary to distinguish between the active
being of the thought or the consciousness and its objective being. There is no such thing as the thought while it
is being a thought, as something that happens; and while
it is happening, it is not an object for itself, it does not
exist for itself. Hence, it is inaccurate to call it thought.
In order that there may be thought, it is necessary for it
to have already occurred and for me to contemplate it
from outside itself, to make of it an object. Then I can
refuse to hold to the conviction which it was for me, refuse to recognize the validity of its existence, and say instead, 'it was an hallucination'; or, to put it more generally,
what was thought in it was internal to it and not an effective reality. This, as we heard earlier, is what is called
thought. Remember that we said, 'When there is only
thought, there is no effective thought of what is being
thought'. When there is only my seeing this wall, there is
no wall. Thought, then, is a conviction that is not in
force; because it is not active but is looked at from outside itself. Thought, then, is an objective aspect which
conviction takes when it no longer convinces. But the
fact is that it adopts that aspect now, that is to say, that it
is my new conviction, that which I now act on, that
which is in force. Only the present conviction, the active

one, is in force, the one that does not yet exist for me; and, therefore, it is not thought, but an absolute position.

Therefore, the idealist thesis which affirms the exclusive reality of thought complicates another, different reality of thought which is the conviction out of which I make that affirmation and within which that affirmation is in force. To put it another way, in order for the idealist thesis, like any other, to be true, it is necessary that the conviction out of which we create this thesis be recognized as in force; that is, that we set forth as absolute reality what this conviction believes there absolutely is. But this is the same as saying that there is reality only when the act of our thinking it does not exist for us, when it is not our object, but when we execute it or are it. So that the condition under which a thesis is firm and solid excludes the very solidity or truth of the idealist thesis.

This makes us recognize that idealism, in trying to establish as a fact what there really is, commits the same error as realism, although in another direction.

Realism's error consists in this; that on determining what is what-there-is, it did not take what-there-is and as it is in its complete purity, but it surreptitiously made an hypothesis—namely, on affirming that what there is are things, in themselves and for themselves, it came to say this: that wall which I see and which, therefore, exists in front of me and is present in front of me will be there when it is not in front of me. In short, it will continue to exist. Is this last not an hypothetical addition and in no way evident? It is indubitable, evident, that the wall exists while it is here in front of me; but it is not beyond doubt that it continues to exist when it is not there in front of me. What there obviously is, then, is the wall before me—therefore, the wall and I, the one and the other, are equally real. And now I am the one who sees the wall, and the wall is that which is seen by me. Consequently, in order for me to be the I that I now am, I have no less need of the wall than it, in order to be what it is, has need of me. Reality is not the existence of the wall alone, and by itself—as realism wished—but neither is it the existence of the wall in me, as my thought, my existence alone and for myself. Reality is my coexistence with the thing.

This—and note it well—does not permit denial that the wall can exist alone and by itself. It is limited to declaring that such ultra-existence, over and above its coexistence with me, is doubtful and problematical. But idealism affirms that the wall is no more than one of my thoughts, that it is only in me, and that I alone exist. This is an hypothetical addition, both arbitrary and problematical. The very idea of thought or consciousness is an hypothesis, not a well-made concept depending beautifully on what there is, as and how it is. The truth is the pure co-existence of an 'I' with things, of things there in front of the 'I'.

Lesson XIV

Revision of the analyzed thesis. Descartes's formula.
The immediate characteristics of doubt. Idealism's nightmare.
Descartes's two courses. Idealism's sleight of hand.
The hypothesis of hallucination. Realism persisting in
idealism; that reality is the independent. Reality is
interdependence and coexistence. The name of basic and
absolute reality in the immediate present . . . living.
Transcendence and immanence of life.

WE ARE SEEKING a basic orientation in our entire surroundings and, therefore, in what there is. For this, we
need to come to agreement with ourselves on what, in
our judgment, there truly is, or what is basic reality. In a
phrase which is more commonplace but also clearer, we
need to put our feet down on something that is completely solid.

We were testing the realist thesis or conviction, according to which reality is things and their grouping, the
world. But this thesis is not firm, for the reason that the
existence of things, insofar as they are separate and independent of the one who thinks them, is problematical and
hypothetical. That this room has an existence in itself,
when it is not present before me, is only an hypothesis
and not a thesis—an hypothesis as probable as you like,
but still an hypothesis, and not a certainty that is evident
or inevitable. But neither can it be considered as probable. The idea of probability has meaning only in reference to a fixed goal: then one can measure and compare
the degree of probability or verisimilitude.

In view of this, we test the thesis which, for the moment, corrects the realist thesis, and we say, 'Reality is

thought, the consciousness of a thing. The existence of that wall in and by itself is problematical, but the present existence of myself seeing that wall is incontrovertible. The wall as seen by me, therefore, not simply as a wall but as my consciousness, my awareness of that wall, is beyond doubt.'

We are studying this idealist thesis from various angles and on several of its dimensions; but now we are going to analyze it in its first classic expression, the one it took in Descartes. We will analyze it at the points that we most urgently need.

As it is well known, Descartes's formula could not be simpler. Nevertheless, if we phrase it in a much more rigorous, more nearly complete, and more advantageous way than the one he used in his texts, we have the following: 'I can doubt the existence of everything except for my own doubt. My doubt is myself doubting; therefore, I cannot doubt my existence. I doubt; therefore, I exist.'

Why cannot one doubt the existence of the doubt? Look at this closely, and do not fall into the error of making the question more complicated than it actually is. The existence of something here means that there really or absolutely is such a thing and not, erroneously that it apparently is or that it may be a matter of opinion. Whether that wall exists or is there, absolutely and not as a matter of opinion, is questionable, doubtful. For the wall to exist absolutely, and for me to think that it exists —these are two different things. On the other hand, for me to believe that the wall exists and for this belief of mine to exist become one and the same thing. It is, then, a matter of the contraposition of two meanings of existence: first, existing in the sense of something existing for me, or my believing that it exists; second, existing as existing in the absolute, and not only for me. Well then, to doubt is nothing but to appear to me that I doubt; therefore, if it seems to me that I doubt, my doubt exists.

Note then, that what makes me unable to doubt the

existence of my doubt is nothing peculiar to the doubt, but that which the doubt has in common with whatever has the characteristic that its absolute existence and its existence for me, or its seeming to me, may be identical.

The discovery made through the genius of Descartes —already touched on by St. Augustine and St. Anselm, but only touched—consists in having noted that 'there is something whose existence in relation to me is identical with its absolute existence; or, to put it another way, there is something whose absolute existence consists in existing for me, or in my belief that it exists'.

This something is doubt, but not doubt alone—also seeing, hearing, imagining, feeling sorrow and pleasure, loving and not loving. What do all these have in common? Simply that these are things of which we are immediately aware, without any intermediary. Of the absolute existence of this wall I can give no immediate account. Between its existence and myself there must intervene my vision, my memory, my thought of it. But between myself and my seeing the wall, there is nothing alien to me that intervenes. If I believe I see, I see; and if I believe I doubt, I doubt.

Well then, says Descartes—not in his *Meditations*, but in a stricter form in his *Principles of Philosophy* (paragraph 9) '*Cogitationis nomine intelligo illa omnia, quae nobis consciis in nobis fiunt, quatenus eorum in nobis conscientia est*'. And in the French translation which he revised, '*Par le mot de penser, j'entends tout ce qui se fait en nous de telle sorte, que nous l'apercevons immediatement par nous-mêmes*'.

Therefore, *cogito, ergo sum.* 'I exist, absolutely', because I am he who believes that he exists. I consist of thought.

Here is the way that Descartes comes to establish the idealist thesis which, in our terminology, sounds like this: the basic reality, that which there truly or absolutely is, is thought.

Can we settle ourselves into this thesis, accept it more or less as the modern age accepted it, and abide by its consequences? Note that these consequences are summarized in this most serious one, which, more than consequence, is the reverse of the thesis itself: If the basic reality is thought, this means that, properly speaking, there is nothing other than thought. Farewell to friends, to things, to the world! All this is, in truth, no more than a swarm of my ideas. I am the blind man who dreamed that he was seeing . . . !

So it is very important that we try to make the terms very clear in order to see if man can at last emerge from the splendid nightmare which idealism has been.

To this end, one must divide Cartesian reasoning into two courses which are very different in value: one which ends in the affirmation that that basic reality is the immediate as such or, what is the same thing, that what truly and absolutely exists is that which exists for me; the other course is composed of a different statement which adds something new and says that immediate reality, that existence of something for me, is thought.

The first course, the thesis of the immediate as basic reality, seems invulnerable. With it, realism is rejected, that is, the opinion which makes reality consist precisely of that which is not immediate to me, of that which does not consist in its existing for me, but on the contrary, in existing for and by itself, in what we customarily call 'things', 'world'. The idealist thesis is firm insofar as it demands that for something to be basic and authentic reality, I must exist with it, that I, too, am in it. When someone tells us a story and we show some doubt of his tale, he usually defends himself by saying, 'I was there'. In effect, man has to be in reality in order that it be reality. A reality from which I am absent is, in essence, problematical and hypothetical. In order not to be questioned, reality must be present and patent. This present and patent being we have called immediacy.

Now, if the immediate—in its immediacy and its presence—we wish to call 'thought', as we might call it 'X', we would have nothing to offer in opposition to the second course of Cartesian reasoning, which is generally idealist.

But the fact is that Descartes and idealism do just the opposite; in calling the immediate 'thought', they introduce into this something which is not in it, something which is not immediate.

Note the definition which Descartes gives of the *cogitatio: 'illa omnia, quae nobis consciis in nobis fiunt'.* Thought is, then, a reality consisting not only and purely in being patent—*nobis consciis*—not only in my being aware of it, but also that *in nobis fiunt*, it is made within us, it has an integral place in us, it *is* us; that is to say, it is *I*. Therefore, thought is a reality which is confined in me, in the subject; it is pure subjectivity.

Now, is this certain? Does the immediate, such and as it shows itself, consist in my being present and patent to myself and nothing more?

Here, I see this wall; my seeing the wall exists absolutely. On the other hand, the existence of the wall, outside of and apart from my seeing it, is problematical. This is the immediate taken in its pure manifestation, in its character as patent, as evident. But now comes the sleight of hand which, in my opinion, idealism practices.

Let us ask ourselves peremptorily, leaving no room for evasion, 'When there is my seeing the wall, what is there?'. Well, there is the absolute reality that I am I, and there is the reality that the wall is to me. When I am seeing it, and while I am seeing it, there is the wall in front of me and for me in exactly the same sense—neither more nor less—as I am there myself. 'Seeing the wall', as the name of a certain immediate situation, does not mean the physiological function of seeing or even the psychological one. On seeing the wall, I do not see either my corporeal seeing nor my psychic or spiritual seeing;

the body is an hypothesis and nothing more; but it is no less an hypothesis that the soul sees. Body and soul are both hypotheses. 'Seeing the wall' does not, strictly speaking, mean more here than the absolute fact that I exist with a wall in front of me which is as existent as I am; it means, then, the coexistence of the wall and my self, but does not in any way mean that whereas I exist absolutely, the wall exists only relatively to me in the sense of being *only* appearance and not effective existence. Why do I exist absolutely? Only for this reason—because I exist for myself. But the same thing happens to the wall; it exists for me as such and, therefore, it exists absolutely.

You will say to me, 'But perhaps you are suffering from an hallucination?'. In the first place, this matter of hallucination is hardly pertinent. Hallucination is the name of an hypothesis of ours with which we are trying to explain certain incongruities in our reality. On the level of the immediate, there are no hallucinations. When I am in a situation which I am then going to describe as hallucinatory—if, for example, we assume that I am now suffering from it—the wall exists as absolutely as when I am enjoying what is considered normal perception. And the fact is that both of these—both hallucination and perception—are concepts which describe not the immediate but a psychophysiological hypothesis. Now we are on an incomparably earlier and more basic level; we are determining the primary reality without having well defined all the rest that remains to be discussed—body, soul, thought, hallucinations, perception.

If, then, by thought, one understands—as is customary in all idealism—a reality in which only the subject, the 'I', exists but nothing else, I deny that the genuinely immediate would be thought. Thought, I repeat again, is a concept which, strictly speaking, means this—that I can bring here before myself that which is really not here because it does not exist. A thing, insofar as it is thought, does not need to exist.

Well now—and this is my decisive judgment in interpreting idealism—the immediate as thought contradicts and makes vulnerable its own and invulnerable point of departure. This consisted in demanding, as a basic and essential characteristic of reality, its immediacy, its palpable presence before me. But the fact is that when I see that wall, it is the wall that is present and patent rather than my seeing it. When I am seeing, I do not see my seeing. In order to observe that there is also the element of my seeing, I must stop seeing and remember that I was seeing a moment ago. I see my seeing when I am away from it, when it is not immediate to me, when the reality which it denoted—seeing the wall—is no longer that reality; I am now in another reality which I call 'remembering something in the past', remembering that I saw the wall.

But if this memory is beautiful, what I will remember as the incident that happened and passed by is that I absolutely existed in front of a wall that also absolutely existed. And if now, for this and other reasons, I find that there is no wall, this—there not being a wall—will be the absolute reality; but it will not be the same absolute reality as before.

How could idealism commit this bit of inconsequential logic with its point of departure which forced it not to recognize as basic reality anything but the immediate? The answer is very simple, for the reason that it keeps within itself, without noting it, the realist tendency. This consisted in believing that the real is that which is independent of the subject, and not that which is, and which exists, dependent on that subject.

Be sure that you understand this thoroughly, because the error of idealism is based precisely on not having understood it. I repeat—realism consists in believing that the real, the truly existent, is what exists independently of me, and not that which exists in a state of dependence upon me. Therefore, it is *that which exists* and not that which does not exist. When idealism sees itself obliged to recognize that this wall exists absolutely as such, and for the precise reason that it depends on me because it is present before me, it does not dare to take things as they offer themselves, but it adds a reasoning and an hypothesis inspired by realism, and says, 'If this wall exists solely insofar and inasmuch as it is present before me, then there is no such wall, but there is a single subject, and the rest is, as it were, contained in it!', or, what is the same thing, there is only thought, subject. Nevertheless, it is more evident than ever that I do not find the wall within myself, but that it is outside of me, there before me; this is at least as clear as that I find myself. And vice versa; never do I find myself alone with myself, but I always find myself certain that I am with something there in front of me which is not myself.

This is not, then, a matter of my sometimes finding the immediate made solely out of my subjectivity and, therefore, of my existing exclusively by myself, but of this— that when I find myself, I always find that self coexisting with something facing that self, something in front of it and opposing it; the world or the circumstance, the surroundings. It is certain that this something does not exist by itself, apart from me. To believe the opposite was the realist error which we have forever overcome. But neither do I ever exist alone and within myself; my existing is coexisting with that which is not I. Reality, then, is this interdependence and coexistence.

When Descartes found that the existence of doubt is indubitable and, therefore, that doubt is a basic or absolute reality, he should have stopped to analyze what it was, in what does the reality called 'doubt' consist? This in place of hurrying to call it 'thought' and with this to falsify it. But—what is there when there is doubt, absolute doubt? There is the I who doubts, and there is that which I find doubtful. In order for there to be doubt, both terms are equally indispensable. And the doubtful thing is not itself doubt, nor is it I, nor subjectivity; but it is something here in front of me which I doubt, and it must exist in order that I, facing it, feel doubt. The 'doubtful' is the characteristic which the world shows me when I doubt, just as 'wall' is the characteristic which the world now presents to me when I look at it.

To put an end to this critique, remember that the first sure path that idealism took consisted in observing that only that exists surely and absolutely which exists for me or in dependence upon me. According to this, in order that 'A' shall exist, it must exist for me. Very well, but it is also necessary that there be an 'A', that it exist as 'A'. If I say that 'A' is a thought of mine, that it is created within me—*in nobis fiunt*—it ceases to be 'A', ceases to exist as 'A'; then one cannot say that it exists for me, that it is dependent on me, but that it is I neither more nor less and, therefore, it is not properly itself. Well now, the truth of the immediate is, as we have seen, the exact opposite. Always, when there is an I, there is something else besides the I, another thing, there in front of me, round about me.

This is why I say that the idealist falls back into a strange realism. In place of leaving the wall to exist with this peculiar characteristic of existing which is being there in front of me, it dissolves the wall into me and makes reality consist in something independent like the realist's reality, except that now the independent element is my thought, is I.

The pure description of the immediate does not allow this; to make thought out of it, to uphold the argument that things are thought, subjectivity, I myself—this is only an hypothesis, as much of an hypothesis as is the realist. It is not the pure thesis of the immediate which is what we lack.

But this obliges us to seek a more adequate concept and a name for that basic and absolute reality which is the immediate. We have said that this always consists in the coexistence of an I with what is not I, with things; these are inseparable from me, and I from them. I exist, but not apart and within myself; but my existing now consists in having this room exist with me. What there truly is, then, is my being with the room and with whatever is clear and patent within it. I do not think this room; my seeing it here in front of me is not a form of thinking it, but is an absolute matter of finding myself with it and in it, an inexorable need to take it into consideration. Well then, that absolute reality which an I must take into consideration something that is not myself, and, therefore, its existing is existing in that other, outside itself—what is this but living? (The outside is the world.)

I do not consist of thinking, in a state of being conscious of this or that. I do not in the first instance think the things I meet. But the reality is that I find myself, first and foremost, among them, with them; I find that they exist and that I also exist. If there is consciousness here, if there is thought, it is a question which does not arise on taking the immediate exactly as it presents itself. On the contrary, because of that absolute brute fact that I now exist and that this wall in front of me exists, I will come later to pose for myself the question of how it is possible that we coexist. This will oblige me to investigate who I am, and, if the answer is that I am an hermetic entity, closed within myself, there will arise the new problem of how, in spite of this, I take account of the wall and all the other things about me. Then, if this should be certain, there would rise up the hypothesis of thought in order to explain how—as nothing from the outside is able to enter into my hermetically-closed being—that wall is, nevertheless, within me.

But this is another of idealism's errors. I am not heremtically closed, but just the opposite. I am that which things penetrate, which they inundate, so much so that they twist me about, sweep me away, contradict me, and destroy me, so that in order to affirm myself in their presence, I must struggle to exert myself, must constantly be doing something with or about them in order to escape their hostility.

If there were only thought, if the idealist thesis were firm and solid, existing would, for me, be solely a matter of being alone with myself. Now, the character of the immediate is just the opposite; I am always outside myself, in the midst of circumstance, of my surroundings. Thought would be a reality without an outside, a pure immanence, an indwelling. The reality of realism is, inversely, a pure outside, without immanence, without any relation to me or any primary dependence on me. Absolute reality, as life, is at once immanent and transcendent. Only that forms part of my life which exists for me, and in that sense it is indwelling. But that immanence does not mean that it is converted into subjectivity, into I myself. *I am not my life. This, which is reality, is composed of myself and of things. The things are not I, nor am I the things. We are mutually transcendent, but we are both immanent in that absolute coexistence which is life.*

The insupportable paradox of idealism is thus overcome without falling back into ingenuous realism. Vice versa, the new thesis keeps both the truth of idealism, which is immanence, and the truth of realism, which is transcendence. That which is not the subject, the not-I, is called transcendent. That wall goes back to being absolutely the wall which all the evidence shows that it is; but it is this not by itself and alone, but as an ingredient of a dual reality whose other ingredient is I myself. My transcendent wall is immanent in my life. My life no more belongs to me than to the wall. In this, it differs from the supposed reality called thought. Thought is mine, is I. My life is not mine, but I belong to it. This is the broad, immense reality of my coexistence with things.